T.D. JAKES

SIX PILLARS FROM EPHESIANS

Overcoming the Enemy

THE SPIRITUAL WARFARE OF THE BELIEVER

ALBURY PUBLISHING
Tulsa, Oklahoma

2nd Printing

Six Pillars From Ephesians: Overcoming the Enemy
The Spiritual Warfare of the Believer
ISBN 1-57778-108-2
Copyright © 2000 by T. D. Jakes
T. D. Jakes Ministries
International Communications Center
P. O. Box 75211
Dallas, Texas 75211

Published by ALBURY PUBLISHING
P. O. Box 470406
Tulsa, Oklahoma 74147-0406

CONTENTS

◎

OVERCOMING THE ENEMY
THE SPIRITUAL WARFARE
OF THE BELIEVER

©

INTRODUCTION

The book of Ephesians is the New Testament equivalent of the Old Testament book of Joshua, and neither one of these books is for wimps! The book of Joshua is a picture of a people who have ceased wandering, come to know their God, embraced the promises of God, and who are now ready to seize what God has promised them.

The book of Ephesians translates the natural warfare of Joshua into the spiritual warfare of the believer. It is not the sort of thing we should read and take to heart unless we are ready to pay the price and do what is necessary to possess all God has for us. This is the book where the apostle Paul commands, "Be strong in the Lord, and in the power of his might!" just as God commanded Joshua, "Be strong and of a good courage!"

I believe we are the Joshua generation.

We are the generation who will storm the gates of hell, take the Promised Land, and bring in the last days' harvest of souls. All unrighteousness will fall to its knees as we proclaim the holy Word of the   Lord.

But have we counted the cost?

Joshua led Israel to take the Promised Land, but he also served Moses patiently and faithfully for forty years in the wilderness, all the while knowing they could have taken the Promised Land just a few months after leaving Egypt. Joshua was one of twelve spies who came back with a good report after observing the land of milk and honey. This is the report Israel rejected, and because of their unbelief, they wandered in the wilderness for forty years. Only Joshua and Caleb believed God.

The Joshua generation will believe God and obey Him.

The Joshua generation will not murmur and complain.

The Joshua generation will give their lives for the Gospel.

The Joshua generation will lay their lives down for their brothers and sisters.

The Joshua generation will not take the glory for themselves.

If we are not willing to pay the price, we will not survive the time of the Joshua generation! We must be tenacious and unyielding in our love for God and for the brethren — and we must know how to war in the spirit.

Warring in the spirit is much more than standing up from time to time and telling the devil to stop hindering our finances or making us sick. Warring in the spirit is defeating all the little foxes that would spoil the vine, little foxes such as greed, lust, jealousy, anger, and fear.

Warring in the spirit is getting up an hour early or staying up an hour later to have that intimate time with the Lord, to hear His instructions for the day, to know His heart and mind, to be empowered with His might, and to be fully clothed in His armor so that the enemy will be driven farther back as we walk in this world.

Warring in the spirit means continually recognizing that we are not warring against people, but the devil and his demons who work through them. Warring in the spirit takes love, faith, patience, faithfulness, and courage — all the characteristics of Joshua.

Joshua was God's warrior, and because he believed and obeyed God, he took the Promised Land.

The Church is Jesus' warrior bride, and when we believe and obey the battle cry of our Lord, we will take the world!

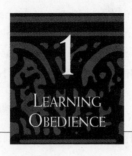

1
LEARNING OBEDIENCE

You need to know something about Joshua if you are going to take the Promised Land: Joshua understood obedience. He lived by God's principle of submission and authority. In fact, every good, effective soldier lives by this principle. No army can wage war successfully without a fighting force that keeps rank and file, respects their officers, and obeys orders. That is why, before Paul dresses us in the armor of God and instructs us in the strategies of spiritual warfare, he explicitly and emphatically tells us in the final verses of Ephesians 5 and the first verses of Ephesians 6 that we must abide in the principle of submission and authority. He explores this vital issue first in the relationship of husband and wife (see Ephesians 5:22-33), which was part of our discussion in *Celebrating Marriage*. I strongly urge you to go back and read our teaching on submission, which will provide more foundation for what we will discuss here with regard to spiritual warfare.

Now, in the first verses of Ephesians 6, Paul continues to talk about submission and authority in context of the relationship between child and parent and then the relationship between slave and master.

CHILDHOOD TRAINING

The mature warrior is an obedient warrior. That's what basic training is about — bringing a civilian's will into line with military standards, military codes, military rules and regulations, and a military way of thinking. If the Church is going to wage war successfully, we must learn to obey our Commander.

Our submission to Jesus Christ is the only relationship in which we know that at all times, under all circumstances, His commands are right and true. There is never a question of His absolute goodness and righteousness. Therefore, our hearts should be continuously submitted to His Word and His Spirit, and our actions should always carry out His will. However, in human relationships, there are times when we are placed in positions where the authority we are submitted to is not right, just, or gentle. Nevertheless, God calls us to these positions for the purpose of working a submissive heart *to Him* in us. As we obey those in authority over us and trust *Him*, we grow in the faith.

God's plan is that we learn obedience as children in the home. As parents lovingly demand that their child's will lines up with their will, they are molding and shaping the child's will to line up completely with the will of the Father for the rest of their lives. Obedience is best learned when a person is a child, young in years. Paul wrote to the Ephesians:

> **C**hildren, obey your parents in the Lord: for this is right.
> Honour thy father and mother; (which is the first commandment with promise;)
> That it may be well with thee, and thou mayest live long on the earth.

EPHESIANS 6:1-3

The adult who was taught obedience by his parents is going to find it much easier to obey the Lord than an adult who was never taught obedience as a child in the home. I firmly believe that a parent who does not teach their child to be obedient is doing their child a great disservice. Structure and order are always much better learned as a child than as an adult. It starts out as simple as setting a rule and holding the child accountable. At 8:00 P.M. Johnny goes to bed — no arguing, no discussion. If Johnny does not obey, he quickly discovers the consequences. If Johnny has an unsubmissive, rebellious, or sour attitude, he finds out immediately that it is unacceptable.

Paul refers to the fifth commandment found in Exodus 20:12 and tells us that this commandment comes with a promise. When we honor our mother and father, we will live a long and prosperous life. If we want our children to live long and prosperous lives, we must teach them to honor us as parents from the moment they are born. We must give them this vital key to life and fulfillment. In addition, it will be so much easier for them to submit to Jesus as their Lord if we teach them to submit to us as babes.

Moreover, a child who is required to show respect for authority at home will have a more enjoyable time with teachers and reap the benefits of learning in school. They will have a natural respect for any adult in authority, whether it is a pastor or a policeman. When they go to work as young adults, they will get along well with their bosses and work well with other employees.

We see one main characteristic again and again in our prison system: These inmates failed to learn respect for authority when they were children. They grew up under one of Satan's most vile and destructive deceptions, believing that their rebellion signified strength and power, that they were their own lords and set their own rules. When you have no respect for authority, you believe the lie that you can do anything and get away with it. You have swallowed the serpent's false doctrine, which he spoke to Eve in the Garden of Eden:

> **N**ow the serpent was more subtil than any beast of the field which the Lord God had made. And he said unto the woman, Yea, hath God said, Ye shall not eat of every tree of the garden?
>
> And the woman said unto the serpent, We may eat of the fruit of the trees of the garden:
>
> But of the fruit of the tree which is in the midst of the garden, God hath said, Ye shall not eat of it, neither shall ye touch it, lest ye die.
>
> And the serpent said unto the woman, Ye shall not surely die:
>
> For God doth know that in the day ye eat thereof, then your eyes shall be opened, and ye shall be as gods, knowing good and evil.
>
> GENESIS 3:1-5

Satan's lie is that we can disobey God and not die, that rebellion against His precepts will make us our own gods, strong and independent. But God's Word tells us that only obedience to God, to parents, to all those in authority over us will bring blessing and joy to our lives. As believers, our hearts submit to God fully when we make Jesus our *Lord*, not just our *Savior*.

Unfortunately, many Christians today have made Jesus their Savior but not their Lord. They are deceived into thinking they can do what they please without consequences because they are saved and going to heaven. Many Christians find themselves halfway through their lives before they recognize who they are in Christ Jesus or realize that, as believers in Christ Jesus, they are to live in total submission to Him. So many people who call themselves Christians are just playing church — they are going through all the motions and saying all the right words, but they have not truly submitted their entire lives to Him so that they are subject to Him in all things. (See Ephesians 5:22,24.)

Obedience is the foundation of who we are in Christ, a key to our success in spiritual warfare, and the lesson of obedience is best learned in our earliest years. It is the sapling — still bendable and pliable — that can best be trained to become a strong tree able to withstand every storm. However, whether we were brought up in the counsel and admonition of the Lord or not, whether we were taught the principle of submission and authority or not as children, right now, before we put on the full armor of God, it is imperative that we submit ourselves completely to Jesus Christ as our Lord as well as our Savior.

Notice that Paul does not command children to *understand* everything their parents tell them to do.

He merely commands them to obey. Paul does not command the Church as a whole to understand all of the mystery in Christ Jesus, nor does he command the believers in Ephesus to understand all of the profound, prolific concepts he illustrates and presents to them. He does require them, however, to obey the truth of God's Word.

This principle holds true for us in every area of our spiritual growth and development, regardless of our age. We must obey those who are more mature in the Lord. We must do what they teach us and command us to do, especially if they hold positions of authority over us. God is a God of principles and concepts. If you learn these principles and concepts, and the principle of submission and authority is one of them, you can apply God's principles to any situation.

For example, one of my first jobs in the church was not to preach, but to play the piano. I figured out right away that once you learned the seven white keys and five black keys, you mastered the entire keyboard. Those twelve notes create an octave which repeats itself over and over to create the keyboard. A similar illustration is our numerical system, which is based upon the numbers zero to nine. If you can count to ten, you can count to a million because the same numbers, with only slight variations in name, repeat themselves over and over.

So it is in the kingdom of God. Jesus taught, "If you are faithful over a few things, I will make you ruler over many things." (See Matthew 25:23.) When God gets ready to teach His people and to raise them up into greater spiritual maturity, He always starts with basic concepts that are readily comprehended and applied. It is for this reason that the Lord admonishes us not to despise small beginnings or the "small things" He does. (See Zechariah 4:9-10.) Anything God originates has the potential to increase, produce a harvest, and be refined into perfection. As we read in Job,

> *Though thy beginning was small, yet thy latter end should greatly increase.*

> JOB 8:7

If you learn to be faithful on one level, you can be faithful on every level. The person who learns how to tithe faithfully on one dollar is a person who is going to tithe faithfully on a million dollars. Those who say they can't afford to tithe have missed the key issues of obedience and faithfulness. They have missed the principles God wants to teach them.

While God is no respecter of *persons* — meaning that He does not favor one person over another —

He is a respecter of *principle*. (See Numbers 23:19) He always upholds His absolutes, and the principle of submission to the Lord is a foundation principle that must be learned before other principles can be built upon it.

GOD'S ORDER

Obedience is bordered by rules, routine, structure, and order. Within the heart and soul of every fallen human being, however, is a natural, fleshly tendency to rebel against these things. Some of us become very subtle in our rebellion, claiming that rules, routine, structure, and order are contrary to the flow of God's Spirit. God's Word, however, states clearly that godly rules, routine, structure, and order are not contrary to the working of the Spirit. (See 1 Corinthians 14.) They make it easier for the Holy Spirit to flow through the Church and for God's people to obey what the Spirit says. Structure and obedience to God's commandments are essential to the work of the Spirit.

In Acts 6 we read about a dispute that arose in the early Church. The apostles responded by appointing seven men of "honest report, full of the Holy Ghost and wisdom" over the practical business of the Church. These seven, called deacons, were to make certain that the needs of all the believers were addressed and met with fairness and equity, while the apostles devoted themselves to prayer and the ministry of the Word. (See Acts 6:1-4.) Seven men were appointed for ministry, and the apostles laid their hands on them and prayed for them. The Church was getting organized, and here was the result:

> **A**nd the word of God increased; and the number of the disciples multiplied in Jerusalem greatly; and a great company of the priests were obedient to the faith.
>
> ACTS 6:7

Structure and order caused the Gospel to go forth with greater effectiveness, more souls were added to the kingdom of God, and even the hardest-to-reach souls — the priests in the Temple — became convinced of the truth about Jesus Christ! Therefore, we can see that requiring obedience of our children is not going to inhibit their creativity or dreams. On the contrary, it will make their creativity and dreams flourish! They will be more useful and effective in God's hands. Requiring obedience of a child will not make the child resistant to the Holy Spirit; it makes the child more sensitive and compliant to the Holy Spirit.

Rules, routine, structure, and order are required if any person is going to learn these basic principles of God:

- Relationships have boundaries, including the relationship of an individual to the greater group or community. Every relationship has boundaries built into it and those boundaries have to be learned and respected. For example, when a person says no to your kisses and hugs, respect that no and back away; or, just because the store is closed doesn't mean you break in to get what you want.

- Respect must be shown for those who make and enforce rules. Every relationship, every culture, every society, and every church is governed by certain rules, written and unwritten. Those rules must be learned. Thou shalt not lie. Thou shalt not commit adultery. Thou shalt not bring food or drink into the main sanctuary. Thou shalt not run in the halls at school. Thou shalt not talk back to the teacher.

- All behavior has consequences. Good behavior brings reward, even though that reward may be only the good feeling and self-respect that come with knowing we have done what is right. Bad behavior brings discipline, chastisement, and punishment. Those who live in accordance with God's Law put themselves in a position to receive God's blessing. Those who routinely and willfully break God's

Law put themselves in a position to be chastised by God, and if they do not repent, they will eventually withdraw from His presence and protection.

Although the Bible does not state it directly, the command to honor your mother and father clearly implies that your days will be lengthened. Therefore, if a child dishonors or disrespects his father and mother, his days will be shortened. As a parent, I would be terrified to train up my children to disrespect me, knowing that because of their disrespect their days would be shortened. We only need to look at the latest edition of any newspaper in this nation to see what is happening to our children when they have no respect or honor for their fathers and mothers. Their lives are being shortened through the violence of the streets and their association with neighborhood gangs who are taking the place of father and mother in their lives.

I want my children to live and I want them to live in blessing. I want them to experience the promise that their respect and honor will cause it to "be well with them." (See Ephesians 6:3.) Not only do I want these blessings and long life for my own natural children, but I also want these things for every "babe in Christ" in my church. I desire to see the entire body of Christ live long and prosperously on the earth.

Why aren't more of God's people experiencing the full blessings of God? Perhaps it is because as new believers in Christ Jesus they aren't taught to respect their elders in the Lord, their spiritual mothers and fathers, and to have a respect for God's authority over their lives. God cannot entrust the full blessings that go with His kingdom to those who do not submit to Him in their hearts and obey Him in their lives.

DO NOT PROVOKE

I love the fact that Paul expresses so clearly God's balance. The exhortation for wives to submit to their husbands is followed immediately by the command that husbands are to love and nurture their wives, to lay down their lives for them. Then the charge to children that they should obey their parents is balanced by God's command to fathers that they "provoke not" their children to wrath. Paul writes,

> **A**nd, ye fathers, provoke not your children to wrath: but bring them up in the nurture and admonition of the Lord.
>
> EPHESIANS 6:4

God's plan for His people is filled with checks and balances. A child must learn to obey and to respect his parents, but at the same time, he is to learn that lesson in an atmosphere of love, kindness, patience, self-control, joy, peace, and mercy. A parent must not be unduly harsh, and never abusive. Such behavior only provokes or prompts a child to imitate the harsh and abusive behavior. A child who is treated with anger is a child who is going to respond with anger.

This passage presents a vivid contrast. One of the definitions of "provoke" is to "send away" or "drive away." Paul says that fathers should not drive away their children to the point of wrath, but bring them up and nurture them in the discipline and instruction of the Lord. To nurture is to love unconditionally and to instruct is to enlighten. We do not just make rules and enforce them. We explain them to our children and discipline them in love.

Pastors, teachers, prophets, evangelists — all who function in roles of authority in the church — must admonish God's people with the same attitude as a loving father in the home. Those who provoke their congregations to wrath by man-made teaching and man-made rules that are harsher than God's Law are going to find they are raising up angry, harsh people. We are to win the world through the manifested strength and power of God's love, not the strength and power of men and women seeking to build their own empires.

Notice that Paul admonishes *fathers* to bring up their children in the nurture and admonition of the Lord. So often in our society, we leave the nurturing of children to mothers. As men, we have a tendency to shirk the responsibility of raising children, saying, "That's a Mama duty." Scripturally, however, we fathers are commanded to love and instruct our children, to raise them up to fear, love, and serve the Lord. This does not mean that a father is to replace the role of a mother in a family, but God expects him to actively contribute and oversee the guidance of his children.

The fact is, children ultimately emulate the authority figure in the home. They learn their value system from the head of the household. Mothers often fight a losing battle trying to instill values and godly behavior in their children by themselves. Those children need to see both their mama's tender devotion to the Lord and their daddy's unshakable commitment to biblical values and godly behavior. Fathers need to become strong advocates of good values in the home, and their children need to know that these values are important to them. This means more than just setting high standards of morality for his family. It means that Daddy lives them before his children so that they can learn godly principles just by watching him.

In the church, the senior pastor is the final authority figure who embodies the values held by the members of the church. If the senior pastor is lax in character, the church will be permeated with undesirable character, no matter how much good may be going on in the various outreaches. The pastor who teaches his people, both in word and by example, to obey the truth of God's Word and fully submit their hearts in a lifestyle of worship before the Lord is a pastor who is going to raise up his "children" to live long and prosperous lives.

These first verses in Ephesians 6 tell us clearly that God is extremely concerned with the training of our children. He wants them to learn early to serve Him and obey His commands because He wants them to live long and be blessed. He knows that the sooner they learn obedience to His will, the sooner they will become mighty men and women of valor in the body of Christ. Then they will do great exploits in the kingdom of God and bring glory to His name.

2

ONE JOB
OPENING

So *Joshua did as Moses had said to him.*

EXODUS 17:10

I'm certain Moses was a great guy, but do you really think he was always great to work for? He had tremendous responsibility and bore the burden of leading millions of very selfish, independent-thinking people. And he had a temper. This is a man who struck the rock and didn't enter the Promised Land because of it! Don't you think there were times when Joshua was just a little bit frustrated, irritated, or aggravated with Moses? And yet the Bible says that Joshua obeyed Moses without complaint. Why? I believe Joshua knew in his heart that one day he would lead Israel across the Jordan to take the Promised Land. He knew God was preparing him for war.

When God created the Church, He gave only one job opening to every member: *slave.* In one New

Testament epistle after another Paul declared that he was merely a servant of the Lord Jesus Christ, but the word he used in the Greek meant "slave." The kind of slave we're talking about here is someone who is utterly and completely devoted to their master. Even if they were offered their freedom, they would refuse it because of their lifelong commitment to their beloved lord. In this same sense, we are all called to be servants of the Lord Jesus Christ.

Pastor . . . slave of the Lord Jesus Christ

Engineer . . . slave of the Lord Jesus Christ.

Parent . . . slave of the Lord Jesus Christ.

Construction worker . . . slave of the Lord Jesus Christ.

Spouse . . . slave of the Lord Jesus Christ.

CEO . . . slave of the Lord Jesus Christ.

Usher. . . slave of the Lord Jesus Christ.

If you're too good for the job, no other openings are available! Jesus made this very clear to His disciples on the night of His betrayal when

> **H**e riseth from supper, and laid aside his garments, and took a towel, and girded himself.
>
> After that he poureth water into a bason, and began to wash the disciples' feet, and to wipe them with the towel wherewith he was girded. . .
>
> If I then, your Lord and Master, have washed your feet, ye also ought to wash one another's feet.

For I have given you an example, that ye should do as I have done to you.

JOHN 13:4-5,14-15

None of us has any justifiable excuse for ever saying, "That job is beneath me" or of thinking, *I'm too good for that job* if we truly want to be warriors for Christ. The only job opening in the kingdom of God is slave!

PLEASING THE LORD

After explaining the importance of submission and authority as it relates to husbands and wives and children and parents, Paul now begins his discourse on the servant and the master.

Servants, be obedient to them that are your masters according to the flesh, with fear and trembling, in singleness of your heart, as unto Christ;

Not with eyeservice, as menpleasers; but as the servants of Christ, doing the will of God from the heart;

With good will doing service, as to the Lord, and not to men:

Knowing that whatsoever good thing any man doeth, the same shall he receive of the Lord, whether he be bond or free.

And, ye masters, do the same things unto them, forbearing threatening: knowing that your Master also is in heaven; neither is there respect of persons with him.

EPHESIANS 6:5-9

Many in Ephesus and other nearby areas had been sold into servitude when Rome invaded their part of the world. In addition to those who were suffering slavery to the Romans, there was a tradition of slavery within the Hebrew community as well. Hebrew men sometimes sold themselves into service in order to repay debts or to acquire something they desired to possess. One of the earliest examples we have of this tradition is Jacob, who became a servant to his uncle Laban in order to gain Rachel as his wife. He worked for Rachel for fourteen years as a servant in Laban's household. (See Genesis 29:1-28.)

Both the Hebrews and the Romans had a number of classes — economic, governmental, and social. As a result, virtually everybody in the early Church served somebody. In this passage of Ephesians, Paul is essentially saying to them and to us, "Refuse to take advantage of your masters and do not rebel against them. Serve them as if you are serving Jesus himself. And masters, do not abuse or mistreat your servants, because Jesus is watching."

Paul knew a great truth about our relationship with the Lord: Regardless of our outer state or circumstances in life, we are servants to Christ Jesus inwardly and eternally free in Him. This is part of the mystery of Jesus and His Church, that as slaves to Christ we are free. Then, because we are called to serve God alone, our service to other people is always "as unto the Lord." We do all of our work for Him, by Him, and in Him. He sees our work and He alone rewards us "according to his riches in glory by Christ Jesus" (Philippians 4:19).

Your employer may be the person who signs your paycheck, but your ultimate Boss is Jesus Christ. He is the one who requires that you be His witness on the job by performing with submission and excellence. He is the one who calls you to the highest standards of morality, integrity, ethics, and godly behavior. He is the one who will convict you that you should not be calling your Grandmama in Chicago on the company phone and pretending she is a client of your company, that you cannot take an hour and a half for lunch and pretend you were only gone thirty minutes! And He is the one who will see your faithfulness and reward you.

There is an interesting verse of Scripture about Joshua that illustrates this very point:

> **A**nd the Lord spake unto Moses face to face, as a man speaketh unto his friend. And he turned again into the camp: but his servant Joshua, the son of Nun, a young man, departed not out of the tabernacle.
>
> EXODUS 33:11 (EMPHASIS MINE)

This scripture indicates that Joshua served Moses, but he looked to God for mercy, justice, blessing, and promotion. Often when we do things for men and women, we naturally expect our reward to come from them. But the Bible says that we are to do all things as unto the Lord and that our reward comes from Him. Nobody may see how much you rehearse for the choir number, but Jesus knows. Nobody may have seen you studying that financial report at 2:00 a.m., but Jesus did. So when you look for your rewards, look to Jesus!

RECEIVING FROM THE LORD

Paul tells us, "Knowing that whatsoever good thing any man doeth, the same shall he receive of the Lord, whether he be bond or free" (Ephesians 6:8). It is the Lord who provides reciprocity for all we do. He is the one who balances the scales and gives us rewards according to our giving, not according to what others think we are worth.

Many Christians get involved in ministries and after a year or two of active involvement, they begin to lose interest and their participation declines. Some of them even lose interest to the point of leaving the church, and a good number of these people give as their excuse, "They were *using* me. They were asking me to do this and give to that and get involved with this and participate in that." My answer to those people is, "Why did you get involved in the church if you weren't available to be used *by the Lord?*" The Lord uses people, and He uses people by asking them to serve other people!

Joshua easily could have complained that he was being "used" by Moses. When Moses stayed on the mountain praying while Joshua was battling Amalek and fighting for his life down below, Joshua may have been tempted to cry, "Moses is using me"! But Joshua submitted to Moses and received special recognition from the Lord as a result:

> *And Joshua discomfited Amalek and his people with the edge of the sword.*
>
> *And the Lord said unto Moses, Write this for a memorial in a book, and rehearse it in the ears of Joshua: for I will utterly put out the remembrance of Amalek from under heaven.*
>
> *And Moses built an altar, and called the name of it Jehovah-nissi.*
>
> EXODUS 17:13-15

God reveals He is our banner of victory in war (Jehovah-nissi) and tells Moses to build the memorial and "rehearse it in the ears of Joshua." He declares that Joshua is the conquering hero of the day. So if anybody comes to you and says you are being "used" in your volunteer work, tell them, "Yes, they are using me! That's what they are supposed to do. I said, 'Lord, I'm available to You and I want to be used.' And the only way He could respond was to use me through somebody. I'm doing what I do as unto the Lord!" This is not just a faith statement; this is a battle cry!

The problem many of us have is that when we do good to our "masters" — whether that person is employer, supervisor, or music minister — we want to reap from the one we have served. If we invest in a company or a ministry or a person, we want to reap from the place we invest. If we don't feel affirmed, appreciated, and rewarded by the person who has "used" us, then we become upset. But the Bible says that our reward comes from the Lord:

> **W**hatsoever good thing any man doeth, the same shall he receive of the Lord.
>
> EPHESIANS 6:8

Anyone who is intensively involved in ministry must ultimately conclude that no person can ever repay them for the sacrifices they make. Only God can reward them adequately for the selfless acts they do on behalf of another. And He does reward us! He says repeatedly in His Word:

> **H**e that cometh to God must believe that he is, and that he is a rewarder of them that diligently seek him.
>
> HEBREWS 11:6

[**J**esus said], *Give, and it shall be given unto you... For with the same measure that ye mete withal it shall be measured to you again.*

LUKE 6:38

[**J**esus said], *But when thou doest alms, let not thy left hand know what thy right hand doeth:*

That thine alms may be in secret: and thy Father which seeth in secret himself shall reward thee openly.

MATTHEW 6:3-4 (EMPHASIS MINE)

Reward and recognition will come from the Father, and He will determine the appropriate reward for us to receive. Now if the Father chooses to reward you richly, don't let anybody make you feel bad about it! Accept whatever it is that the Lord provides for you, great or small. Keep giving the same faithful, humble, and excellent service regardless of how much He puts into your hand or how much praise you receive. The more the Lord proves that He can trust you with His blessings, the more He will bless you. And all along the way, whether you are abased or are abounding, choose to be content and to serve cheerfully. This is an act of faith in God and God alone.

When an army goes into battle, all lives are on the line. The sergeants may be making more money than the privates, even though the privates may be taking a greater risk. Not every paycheck in the military is the same. This is also true in God's kingdom. Some receive thirtyfold returns, others receive sixtyfold returns, and still others receive hundredfold returns. (See Matthew 13:3-8.) The rate of return is up to the Father. Our part is to be grateful for whatever He gives us, to expect His reward, to receive it gratefully, and to stop looking to other people to compensate us for what we sacrifice on their behalf.

Our motivation for serving the Lord must never be the material return we are anticipating. Our motivation must be our love for the Lord. Any material return is a fringe benefit He allocates to our lives. The real value of what we give is measured back to us in things eternal that cannot be measured on this earth.

KINDHEARTED MASTERS

The same balance the Lord gives for husbands and wives or parents and children is stated in the relationship that masters are to have with their servants. Paul writes:

> *Ye masters, do the same things unto them, forbearing threatening: knowing that your Master also is in heaven; neither is there respect of persons with him.*
>
> EPHESIANS 6:9

Those who are in a position of authority must never take advantage of the people who serve under their leadership. There is no place in God's kingdom for leaders who are domineering, vengeful, or motivated by anger or hatred for any individual or group of people, at any time or under any circumstances.

I personally believe that no person should ever be appointed to leadership until they have learned to follow. A good leader will be a person who was a good follower. They understand the difficulties and challenges of serving someone as unto the Lord. If they have learned to serve people as unto the Lord, when they are at the top of the human leadership ladder, they will still follow the leadership of the Lord. In this position, more than ever before they must be able to hear, submit to, and obey the leading of the Holy Spirit.

Joshua was a great leader because he was a faithful servant to Moses for many years. He remembered the difficulties of submitting to a flawed human being when he himself became the leader. Any time a person does not know what it's like to walk in the shoes of another person, the possibility exists for an abuse of power and for abusive behavior. For God to trust us with positions of authority, we must prove first that we know how to control our own desires and lusts for recognition, fame, and power. God-appointed leaders never lead by threat or force; but rather, they lead through the compelling combination of love and righteousness.

What about those who find themselves in a situation where the master is abusive? Should they rebel? No. Paul states clearly that servants should obey their masters "with fear and trembling, in singleness of your heart" (Ephesians 6:5). Is that a vulnerable position? Yes! But the person who chooses to remain submissive will be vindicated by God. Joshua learned this when he witnessed the deliverance of Israel from Pharaoh. God will remove any leader who consistently abuses His children.

It is dangerous to rebel against authority. Moreover, you can obey outwardly and still have an unsubmissive heart, which is still rebellion in God's eyes. Remember, God is interested in the heart, because if He has your heart He has *you*. On the other hand, you can submit in your heart and refuse to obey if your employer requests you to do something against the Word of God. But you must remain submissive to the one in authority while you respectfully refuse to obey. Why? Maintaining a submissive heart and attitude is simply staying in fellowship with the Lord and doing His will. If you do not remain submissive inwardly, God will have to deal with your rebellious heart and chastisement will occur not only for the abuser but for you.

Obviously, if the abuse is placing you in danger physically, emotionally, or spiritually, you must pray about quitting. Rest assured, however, eventually God will remove the abusive leader. I have seen God remove people from leadership in all kinds of ways. When Pharaoh abused the children of Israel and refused to repent, God drowned him. I have also seen Him rescue the abused in all kinds of ways. He removed the Israelites from the abuse of Pharaoh with signs, wonders, and miracles.

Again, I cannot emphasize this strongly enough: It is a dangerous thing for those in authority to abuse a child of God. When a child of God is abused, the Lord will hear and respond to their distress. He will send a strong deliverer to set them free!

LIKE JESUS

Just as soldiers must obey their commander, every believer is called to obey the Lord — and not occasionally, but continually. We do not obey only when the circumstances seem right or when we like the person in authority, but we obey all those in authority over us as if we were obeying the Lord himself. Peter taught us a hard truth in his first epistle:

Submit yourselves to every ordinance of man for the Lord's sake: whether it be to the king, as supreme;

Or unto governors, as unto them that are sent by him for the punishment of evildoers, and for the praise of them that do well.

1 PETER 2:13-14

We are to submit to the laws of men as though God himself had written them. We are to submit to all those in authority over us because God has set them in those positions. To rebel against them is to rebel against God. And if they require anything ungodly or unscriptural of us, we are to disobey outwardly but remain submissive inwardly. In this way our hearts stay pure before the Lord and our obedience to Him is complete.

Unfortunately, most of us probably rebel more for selfish reasons than scriptural convictions. We're in a hurry so we break the speed limit. Our boss is an insensitive tyrant and doesn't pay us what we're worth, so we add an hour here and there on our overtime. We believe the income tax is unconstitutional and oppressive, so we don't report the cash we received for doing odd jobs.

This rebellion and lawlessness is too common in the local church. We don't like the songs the choir director chooses so we quit the choir, even though God has called us there to learn submission to *that* choir director. So then we get involved in outreach, but the director of outreach is disorganized. We get so frustrated with their lack of administrative ability that we eventually quit that too. The truth is, we will go from one endeavor to the next until we learn to submit to authority, stop complaining, and do all things as unto the Lord. We will never be content until we master our selfish whims, put aside our personal agendas, and simply obey God by serving those He has set in authority over us.

When God places us under authority that is not pleasant or does not operate as we would operate, we know He is working on our level of submission to authority! He is preparing us for battle! He is showing us how to lay down our lives! If we are to be like Jesus in this earth, we must learn obedience to the point of crucifying our self and our flesh. Jesus poured His life out for us in obedience to the Father, and His example is the model we are to follow. We are to pour our life out for others in obedience to God.

If we are set in authority over others, we must pour our lives out in obedience to God more than ever. God will impart an anointing for us to lead, instruct, and set an example; but we must be even more sensitive and submissive to the Holy Spirit, carrying out our responsibilities with fear and trembling. Our leadership must bear the hallmarks of both the confidence and humility of Christ.

Obedience enables us to be all God designed us to be. It frees our potential and releases our ministries. But most importantly, when we learn obedience, we learn the foundation for waging war and winning. The enemy will face a formidable fighting force when our army of Christian soldiers obey those in authority and our officers model Jesus to those they lead. We will be of one mind, one heart, and one spirit, and nothing will cause us to break rank. The gates of hell shall not prevail against God's obedient Church.

3

BE STRONG
AND STAND

Finally, my brethren....

EPHESIANS 6:10

Finally... Paul has come to the crux of the matter, the place to which he has been leading us for five and a half chapters. He has revealed our incredible wealth in chapter 1, the rich treasury we have in Christ Jesus. He has shared some of the deep secrets of the kingdom, that we are chosen in Christ Jesus from the foundation of the world, adopted into the family of God, and accepted in the beloved. He tells of our marvelous redemption and God's workmanship in our lives in chapter 2. We are made alive by the blood of Jesus, no longer bound by guilt and condemnation, and Gentile and Jew are one in Him. We are saved and being saved every day by His grace, seated with Him in the heavenlies, and the enemy is under our feet.

Then, in chapter 3, Paul begins to teach us how we are strengthened in our inner man by the power of the Holy Spirit, that our response to all God has done for us is to "bow our knees to the Father." (See Ephesians 3:14.) He addresses our worship unto God and explains that a constant attitude of worship releases God's holiness, power, and glory in our lives. Then, in chapters 4 and 5, he turns our attention to our walk, that we are to walk worthy of the calling God has placed on our lives, not just witnessing *about* Jesus, but *being* a witness to those around us that Jesus is our Lord.

In chapter 5 Paul explores our role as the submissive bride of Christ and talks about our wedding to Christ Jesus. Then he continues to firmly instruct us in the principle of authority and submission in chapter 6, using the examples of children and parents, and masters and servants. By the time we come to Ephesians 6:10, we are perfected for ministry and corporately edified, unified, and made doctrinally wind-resistant. Now, Paul is going to tell us the point of everything we have learned and all the training we have been through: God has prepared us for spiritual warfare.

STRONG IN THE LORD

After Moses died and Joshua became the leader of the children of Israel, God commanded Joshua to take the Promised Land and assured him of victory.

Then He proceeded to command Joshua, not once but several times, to "be strong and of a good courage" (Joshua 1:6). The apostle Paul reiterates the same command to the Church in Ephesians 6:10:

> *Finally, my brethren, be strong in the Lord, and in the power of his might.*

Being "strong in the Lord" is not an option in the kingdom of God! We are commanded to be strong because every believer is involved in intense spiritual warfare, every day, in all areas of life. The original text translated "Finally" is *tou poilou*, which means "to the rest" or "as for what remains for you to do." What remains for the Church to do? We must "be strong in the Lord, and in the power of his might." We are chosen and prepared to do battle against all enemies of the kingdom of God. Finally — after Egypt and after the wilderness — we are matured and empowered to fight the good fight of faith!

The war in the spirit realm is an ongoing battle between the Lord Jesus Christ and Satan, and we are the body of Christ on this earth. Therefore, Satan is the enemy of our souls. Before we were saved, he hated us because we were made in the image of God, but we were under his control. Now that we have received Jesus as our Lord and Savior and entered the kingdom of God, we are a threat to Satan's rule on earth. Jesus gave us authority over him! Paul is saying, "Finally, my brethren, it is time to use the authority you have through the blood of Jesus. This is a war from which you cannot and must not back down!"

As the Joshua generation, we are a warring bride, a fighting Church, a possessing Church that combats the adversary. We are taking back what rightfully belongs to the kingdom of God. There's no escaping the fight, not because we are a vengeful, hateful, warring people, but because the enemy of our souls is vengeful and hateful and warring in nature. We engage in spiritual warfare because Satan opposes every step we take into the Promised Land. God has given His people a vision and a hope and a future which is sure, but His people must fight to possess all He has given.

At this point you may be asking, "Why does our loving heavenly Father make us fight for the blessing?" I firmly believe there are some things about God we cannot know or understand until we go through some struggles with His help and on His behalf — and He knows it. He knows that we will only learn and appreciate the keeping power of His Word and seek the guidance of His Spirit when we are in the middle of a strong battle. In the crucible of crisis, suddenly something we read or studied weeks or months ago appears in our thinking at just the right moment to give us hope and faith for that particular time and place.

It all begins with a vision, a dream, a word from God that lays the foundation and sets the compass for our life. Just as He sent Joshua into the Promised Land to spy out all that had been given Israel, he gives us a foretaste of the thing He desires to give us, and He shows us how much we will enjoy it. He shows us that He is going to do great and mighty things in our lifetime and that His provision is already on the way. And then all hell breaks loose! We cry out, "Lord, I thought the prophecy was that I was going to fulfill this great calling in Your name, that the windows of heaven were opening to me, and that together we were going to do great exploits. Well, I crossed the Jordan like You told me to, but all I see is this great, impenetrable wall!"

If we had to summarize one principle related to the receiving of God's blessings, it would be this: *Not without a struggle.* Whatever God shows us, speaks to us, puts in our spirit, or whatever has been prophesied to us about our ministry, our life, our finances, our children, our marriage, our grandchildren, we must understand that it will not happen without a struggle on our part.

The Lord may show us Jericho and tell us it is ours, but we still must march around seven times, shout, and then defeat the inhabitants once the wall is down. (See Joshua 6.) The Lord may show us a land flowing with milk and honey and say to us, "This is yours," but it will still be up to us to rid the land of God's enemies before we can settle down to eat the grapes. (See Numbers 13:1-14:25.)

We can learn about the full wealth that belongs to us in Christ Jesus, but in order to obtain it, we are going to have to learn the skills of spiritual warfare. We are going to have to roll up our sleeves and do some hand-to-hand combat with the enemy of our souls if we are going to drive the enemy away from our blessing and claim it as our own.

You may be going through some things right now, and you're saying, "Lord, what in the world am I going to do? My finances are under attack. My marriage is under attack. My reputation is under attack." This is what you're going to do: Be strong in the Lord, and in the power of His might!

Unfortunately, this generation of believers has been taught that anything that comes against us can just be removed, gotten around, or cast out. We hear, "You don't have to take it. You're a Christian. You have authority!" There you are, a Christian, which means your whole foundation is built on a Man who had to endure beatings, whipping, all manner of verbal and physical abuse, and then crucifixion. Once, He turned to His disciples and said, "If you're going to follow Me, you have to take up your cross. If they persecuted Me, they will persecute you. There is a price you must pay for the Gospel." How can the cross symbolize and epitomize our faith if we teach that when we have enough faith, we don't have to have the cross?

The strength of God is not proven in how much we cast away. *The strength of God is proven in how much we endure.* Jesus proved His strength when they nailed Him to the tree and He kept preaching with nails in His hands. Stephen didn't stop the stoning, but forgave his persecutors, looked up, and worshipped Jesus while stones were beating him in the head. This is being strong in the Lord and in the power of His might!

This generation of the Church in America has not endured much of anything. It's going to be embarrassing when many of us get to heaven and gather with the saints of the ages. They will talk about being beheaded, skinned alive, boiled to death, tortured, and seeing their whole family executed. Then we will say, "Somebody talked about me so bad. We were really up against it because we had to go to the bank three times to get the loan. They didn't support me in the choir when I sang my song. I was in charge of the spaghetti dinner and no one would bring salad." These things are not suffering for the Lord!

In this country, we think suffering for the Lord is fanning ourselves because the air conditioners went out in the service. Suffering for the Lord is not getting our parking spot and having to walk all the way across the parking lot to get to church. In a testimony service in heaven, would we have anything significant to say? How dare we complain about these light afflictions! If we don't get busy, we're not going to have anything to say in heaven. We'll be on the back row, over in the corner with our head down, saying, "Thank You, Lord, for letting me in. I'm just glad to hang out with these good brothers and sisters."

We are to take up our cross and go forward. But when we fight to possess the promises of God and fulfill His calling, the scripture verse we are studying says that we are not to fight in our own strength:

> **F**inally, my brethren, be strong in the Lord, and in the power of his might.
>
> EPHESIANS 6:10 (EMPHASIS MINE)

Anytime a person attempts to go into battle against spiritual forces in their own strength, they invite disaster into their lives, setting themselves up for heartache and failure. The Greek language in this verse gives us a key to receiving the strength of the Lord. The phrase "be strong" is derived from the Greek word *dunamis*, which means power. Many

48

Christians have heard this Greek word, but in this case, knowing the form of the word is important because it is a verb in the passive voice, *endunamoo*, which means "empowering." What this means is that the action of the verb, "empowering" or "making strong," is being done to us by God. Paul is saying, "Allow God to fill you with His power."

The image here is not of an athlete who has become strong because he has done push-ups, sit-ups, and lifted weights. Such athletes would be strong by their own efforts. No! Believers who are strong become so because they receive the literal strength of God from God. They are allowing God to empower them with His strength and might.

The phrase "the power of his might" is full of meaning also. The words "power" and "might" are *kratos* (intensity of the power) and *ischus* (the power itself). We could translate these words as, "Finally, allow yourselves to be made strong by the power of His power." Literally, "the power of His might" is like saying the "wetness" of water, the "sweetness" of sugar, or the "blinding brilliance" of light. We must allow the Lord to empower us with the very essence and substance of His power.

However we translate this verse, Paul is talking about a lot of power!

IT'S A BIG PUT-ON

It's one thing for Paul to tell us, "Just allow God to fill you with His power," and it's another thing to know how to allow God to do that. Do we just get in our prayer closet, close our eyes, and say, "Do it, God"? I don't know about you, but I need a little more explanation of this process. Thank God, the Holy Spirit gives it to us.

Put on the whole armour of God, that ye may be able to stand against the wiles of the devil.

EPHESIANS 6:11

As an act of our will, we are to allow God to empower us by suiting up in His armor. Only then can we hold our ground when the devil assaults us. We stand immovable and unshakable against the attacks of the enemy and defeat him with God's power and might when we put on the armor of God.

The truth is, we don't have any idea what we look like in God's armor or what it can do until we put it on. Most of us have gone shopping for clothes, and we look through racks and racks of different things. We know, however, that until we take that new outfit back to the dressing room, remove everything that goes with the old outfit, and actually put on the new clothes, we are never going to get a true picture of what it will look like.

The same is true for spiritual clothes. We must take off the old man to fully see and appreciate the new man. We must take off every natural piece of armor to fully see and appreciate our godly spiritual armor. Paul describes this casting-off-and-putting-on process in a number of his letters:

> *The night is far spent, the day is at hand: let us therefore cast off the works of darkness, and let us put on the armour of light.*
>
> ROMANS 13:12

> *For as many of you as have been baptized into Christ have put on Christ.*
>
> GALATIANS 3:27

To put on the *whole* armor, we must strip off every warring device of the carnal man, every weapon and strategy of the flesh we have used to engage in natural fights, overcome natural obstacles, and endure natural phenomenon. We must put off our own ideas and strategies and put on God's armor and strategies for fighting in the spirit realm.

We must take off lies and put on truth.

We must put away sin and put on righteousness.

We must cast off guilt and death and put on salvation and eternal life.

We must get rid of strife and put on peace.

We must put off doubt and unbelief and put on faith.

We must put away ignorance and put on knowledge of the Word.

Every piece of spiritual armor is vital, and no piece of the old natural armor can be retained because none of it is suitable for the spiritual fight ahead. The old weaponry and strategies are only going to weigh us down, slow us down, and cause us to stumble in the heat of battle.

It's almost difficult to fathom that this is the same Paul who, just a few verses before in chapter 5 of Ephesians, wrote about our intimacy with the Lord. We enjoy the gentle embrace of Jesus as He holds His bride tenderly in His arms, our head laying on His breast, covered by His love and protection. Now, suddenly, we are moved from the warmth of His touch to the battlefield of the soul! But friend, that's the way life is: One minute you are worshipping God with ecstasy and the next you are in the heat of spiritual battle. And it's all God! He's the God of warm and intimate embrace and He's the God of fierce and enduring battle — and you cannot win a spiritual battle without being intimate with the Lord.

Think again of our analogy of the dressing room, which is a private place in which we can put on new clothes. Lying in the arms of our Bridegroom is our spiritual dressing room, the place we become strong in the Lord and in the power of His might.

In the secret place of the Most High, under the shadow of Almighty God is the private place where we put on His armor and receive our battle plan. *We must be the bride of Christ to become a warring Church!*

STAND, STAND, STAND

The very idea of armor evokes the picture of imminent war, battling, fighting, and life-and-death conflict. There's no need for armor unless we are in immediate danger of being injured or destroyed by an enemy. The armor Paul tells us to put on is armor aimed at diverting a disaster. We must wear this armor if we intend to stand against the onslaught of the devil.

> **P**ut on the whole armour of God, that ye may be able to stand against the wiles of the devil.
>
> EPHESIANS 6:11

I find these words of Paul extremely encouraging. For the Lord to tell me to put on armor that I might stand indicates to me that I'm in the right spot. When the time comes for the Lord to tell me to suit up for a fight, the Lord has me precisely where He wants me to be. It's as if He walked me right up to my destiny and said, "We're here on the edge of your Promised Land. Don't let any of the things you see make you think that what lies ahead of you isn't for you. Don't look at how high the wall is or how many enemy chariots you see. Don't see how many problems are coming against you. Don't focus on your inner weaknesses and fears. I've brought you here. Now all you have to do is to suit up in my armor and stand until the land is yours!"

To stand is to both obtain and maintain what God has given us. We must never enter a spiritual battle thinking that we simply need to fight it and win it and never think about it again. Once we have obtained a promise of God, we must continue to stand strong in the power of His might in order to maintain our position and blessing.

Don't let the wind blow you this way and that or move you to the left or the right. Don't let the cunning persuasion of men sway you from your spot. Once God has placed you in a position, stand there until He calls you to move forward. Celebrate your victory, but never let down your guard. You must continue to stand if you intend to keep what God has given you!

Paul had some interesting things to say about Satan's attempts to break him,

> **A**nd now, behold, I go bound in the spirit unto Jerusalem, not knowing the things that shall befall me there:
> Save that the Holy Ghost witnesseth in every city, saying that bonds and afflictions abide me.

> But none of these things move me, *neither*
> *count I my life dear unto myself, so that I might finish*
> *my course with joy, and the ministry, which I have*
> *received of the Lord Jesus, to testify the gospel of the*
> *grace of God.*

ACTS 20:22-24 (EMPHASIS MINE)

Even though Paul knew great trials awaited him if he continued his call to preach the Gospel, he refused to be dislodged from his spot in the Lord. He was fully girded up in the armor of God, and he refused to be moved from the territory He had given him. He refused to give in and return to a reliance upon fleshly desires and human caution. He refused to be constrained by a desire to take it easy and let others carry the banner of the Gospel.

God calls and equips us and empowers us to progress, but He also calls us to stand in our faith, fully clothed in His armor, so that we don't digress. It is up to us to stand in the land where He has placed us until He calls us to move forward and claim more land. The armor is God's, but the stand is ours. Armor doesn't stand up by itself! We stand in the armor.

Furthermore, there's no need to put armor on a person who is running away! God's armor is for those who are going to stand and defend those things that are truly important to them. Is there anything today that God has given you about which you feel strongly enough to stand with all your faith? That's the stuff you want the armor for! The armor God gives you is used to stand against the enemy so that he cannot take back what God has already given to you in the spirit realm.

Are you willing to stand for your eternal salvation and the gift of the Holy Spirit within you?

Are you willing to stand for your peace?

Are you willing to stand for the salvation of your children?

Are you willing to stand for your marriage and your family?

Are you willing to stand for the opportunity to preach the Gospel?

Are you willing to stand for the ministry the Lord has given to you?

In case you are questioning the importance of standing, notice how many times Paul repeats the word "stand" in this passage about spiritual warfare:

> **P**ut on the whole armour of God, that ye may be able to stand *against the wiles of the devil.* . . .
>
> *Wherefore take unto you the whole armour of God, that ye may be able to* withstand *in the evil day, and having done all, to* stand.
>
> Stand *therefore.*
>
> EPHESIANS 6:11,13-14 (EMPHASIS MINE)

As for me and my house, we will choose to be strong in the Lord, then stand and keep on standing!

4

KNOW YOUR FOE

Most of us in the body of Christ know who we are fighting in the spirit realm. Whether we call him the devil, Satan, or the evil one, he is the enemy of the Lord Jesus Christ and of our own souls. What many of us do not know is where and how he strikes. We don't know his tactics. We don't understand the spirit realm in which he operates. But if we are going to defeat him, we need to know where and how the enemy works.

WHERE IS THE ENEMY?

When Joshua began his campaign to conquer the Promised Land and faced the formidable wall of Jericho, Jesus appeared to him and said,

> **A**nd it came to pass, when Joshua was by Jericho, that he lifted up his eyes and looked, and, behold, there stood a man over against him with his sword drawn in

his hand: and Joshua went unto him, and said unto him, Art thou for us, or for our adversaries?

And he said, Nay; but as captain of the host of the Lord am I now come. And Joshua fell on his face to the earth, and did worship, and said unto him, What saith my lord unto his servant?

And the captain of the Lord's host said unto Joshua, Loose thy shoe from off thy foot; for the place whereon thou standest is holy. And Joshua did so.

Now Jericho was straitly shut up because of the children of Israel: none went out, and none came in.

JOSHUA 5:13-6:1

Then Jesus gave him explicit instructions about how to take the city, which was heavily fortified:

And the Lord said unto Joshua, See, I have given into thine hand Jericho, and the king thereof, and the mighty men of valour.

And ye shall compass the city, all ye men of war, and go round about the city once. Thus shalt thou do six days.

And seven priests shall bear before the ark seven trumpets of rams' horns: and the seventh day ye shall compass the city seven times, and the priests shall blow with the trumpets.

And it shall come to pass, that when they make a long blast with the ram's horn, and when ye hear the sound of the trumpet, all the people shall shout with a great shout; and the wall of the city shall fall down flat, and the people shall ascend up every man straight before him.

JOSHUA 6:2-5

The Bible records that when Joshua did exactly as Jesus commanded, the wall of Jericho fell down flat and the city was Israel's. Thank God, Jesus is our Captain too! He knows how to gain the victory over all the demons because He crushed them at the resurrection. Earlier in the book of Ephesians, Paul declared that Jesus overcame death and was raised and seated "far above all principality and power and might and dominion and every name that is named." He is the Warrior who defeated all enemies and "put all things under his feet." (See Ephesians 1:19-22.)

Jesus revealed to Joshua that Jericho would be his when the wall came down, and Joshua understood that the wall was merely the key that unlocked the city. Let me tell you two things about your problems and the challenges that stand between you and the promises of God that are yours. *First, your promise is locked up behind a problem.* A problem is nothing but a door to a promise. Don't allow the problem to intimidate you from getting the promise! The promise is yours to possess. It's simply trapped behind a wall like Jericho, and Jesus is your wall-toppling Captain!

Second, you must fight when Jesus tells you how to unlock the promise. He knows it and you need to recognize it. You need to know there will be a struggle, and you cannot be paralyzed or discouraged by that fact. You need to know that the fight will take place and you have no need to fear. How can you know you are about to engage in a struggle and not be afraid? Because your faith is in Jesus Christ, the Living Word of God!

> **T**hrough faith we understand that the worlds were framed by the word of God, so that things which are seen were not made of things which do appear.
>
> HEBREWS 11:3

God is saying to us that everything we call physical was manifested from something spiritual. We also understand that the spiritual reality becomes physical reality as the Word of God is spoken in faith. The promises of God are ours the moment we believe them in our hearts and then confess them in faith. Jesus declared this principle of the kingdom of God:

> **A**nd Jesus answering saith unto them, Have faith in God.
>
> For verily I say unto you, That whosoever shall say unto this mountain, Be thou removed, and be thou cast into the sea; and shall not doubt in his heart, but shall believe that those things which he saith shall come to pass; he shall have whatsoever he saith.
>
> Therefore I say unto you, What things soever ye desire, when ye pray, believe that ye receive them, and ye shall have them.
>
> MARK 11:22-24

Right now we must recognize that we live simultaneously in two spheres of existence — the spiritual realm and the natural realm — and our enemy is in the spiritual realm. The spiritual realm is the "parent" realm from which everything natural is given birth. The natural realm is an outworking of the spiritual realm. Therefore, if we are to be successful in defeating the enemy, we must defeat him in the spiritual realm. Then the natural realm will fall in line with what has been accomplished in the Spirit.

At every moment and in every situation, Jesus knows where the enemy is and what he is doing to try to wreak havoc in the body of Christ. Our challenge is to follow Jesus in the Spirit and stop the devil before he even gets started!

WHO IS THE ENEMY?

> Put on the whole armour of God, that ye may be able to stand against the wiles of the devil.
> For we wrestle not against flesh and blood, but against principalities, against powers, against the rulers of the darkness of this world, against spiritual wickedness in high places.
>
> EPHESIANS 6:11-12

Our Bridegroom is issuing a battle cry to His Warrior Bride, and that cry is not against people, but against spiritual evil. One thing we must always remember about spiritual warfare is that our battle is against the enemy of our souls, Satan and his demonic forces. We are never against people, particularly our brothers and sisters in Christ. Although the enemy may manifest himself through human beings, our warfare is against the principalities, the powers, and the rulers of darkness that are causing evil behavior.

Believers are in a deadly wrestling match with principalities, powers, and the rulers of the darkness of this world. "Principalities" is the Greek word *archas*, which means rulers and authorities, in this context speaking of the demonic realm. The *Bauer's Lexicon* (see References at the back of the book) states that this term points to the existence of a political organization in the demonic realm, a hierarchy of ranking demons who have authority over territories.

"Powers" is translated from *exousia*. While this word is used in Scripture for ability, it most often implies authority. Paul is telling us that within the political hierarchy of demonic beings, some have authority over others. Then we have the "rulers," *kosmoscrators*, who are literally world rulers of this darkness. The text here is not referring to government officials, kings, or dictators. This passage peers into the spiritual realm where these rulers preside over the "darkness of this world," or Satan's kingdom. You might call these evil territorial spirits.

This evil hierarchy makes life miserable on planet earth. No matter what people do to us, we must be mindful that they are not our enemy, and we are never to seek revenge or restitution. We are to forgive our offenders, turn them over to God, and look to Him for justice and mercy. Throughout the Scriptures we find admonitions that our battle belongs to God and that He alone exacts vengeance:

> **D**early beloved, avenge not yourselves, but rather give place unto wrath: for it is written, Vengeance is mine; I will repay, saith the Lord.
>
> ROMANS 12:19

> **F**or we know him that hath said, Vengeance belongeth unto me, I will recompense, saith the Lord. And again, The Lord shall judge his people. It is a fearful thing to fall into the hands of the living God.
>
> HEBREWS 10:30-31

So how do we battle when people hurt and wound us, defraud us, and seek to destroy us in some way? The wiles of the devil are mental attacks. He assaults our minds with evil, deceptive thoughts and counts on the fact that we will believe these to be our thoughts and will accept them as truth. Primarily, our battle is fought in the mind.

The Greek word "wiles" is *methodeias*, which means "trickery." This word covers evil thinking, evil strategies, and evil motivations. Because Satan was utterly defeated and rendered powerless at the cross and resurrection of Jesus Christ, he must persuade us that he has power and deceive us into seeing and doing things his way. Therefore, in order to control our wills, he and his demons direct their trickery toward our minds.

The devil seeks to turn us against people while he hides in the shadows of deception. You've probably experienced this many times, usually without knowing it. You're troubled about something, and you don't even know what it is. You drive around and around, but you don't know where you're going. The devil introduces an entire thought process that will convince you that your problem is your boss. He's working you too hard. He doesn't understand you. Your work is valueless and unappreciated. And you become obsessed with this horrible situation.

In reality, you're not fighting with flesh and blood, with your boss, but with demons of restlessness and fear who are making you believe lies to get you to abort God's will for your life. If you don't stop those thoughts dead in their tracks and cast down the vain imaginations, you will do something completely contrary to God's will and plan for your life. You will hurt yourself and others.

What will keep you straight and focused in spiritual warfare is to remember at all times that people are not your enemy. Your battle is with Satan and his demonic forces.

HOW DOES THE ENEMY OPERATE?

> **P**ut on the whole armour of God, that ye may be able to stand against the wiles of the devil.
>
> For we wrestle not against flesh and blood, but against principalities, against powers, against the rulers of the darkness of this world, against spiritual wickedness in high places.
>
> EPHESIANS 6:11-12

Have you watched any wrestling matches lately? When you wrestle someone, your body is pressed against theirs. All your strength and knowledge of the sport is concentrated on pinning your opponent so that they cannot move and are rendered powerless. When the apostle Paul spoke of wrestling to the Ephesians, however, he described a hand-to-hand, face-to-face combat that proved to be a brutal end for the loser. In the Roman Empire, the loser had his eyes gouged out! By using this word Paul is clearly saying, "You've got to know what you're doing because you cannot lose this battle!" We are in a wrestling match with an enemy whose sole intent is to steal, kill, and destroy us. (See John 10:10.)

We need to know that the devil is not impulsive in his attacks against us. *Methodeias* means he develops strategies, plans, and schemes. He calculates his moves, anticipates our counter moves, and waits patiently, like the snake he is, to strike us at our weakest moment. That is why it seems he always attacks us when we're down. He attacks when he feels it will have the maximum impact. He wants to stop us dead in our tracks. He wants our vehicles to run out of fuel, our soldiers to run out of resolve, our weapons to run out of ammunition, and our faith to fizzle out.

Yes, we have been given authority over Satan and his evil demonic cohorts through the name and the blood of Jesus Christ, but we must never underestimate their cunning craftiness and trickery. They've been around a lot longer than we have and are a lot smarter than we are! Our natural understanding, therefore, is worthless against their knowledge and ability. That is why we must put on the armor *of God* and stand in the strength *of the Lord.* We cannot fight and win a spiritual war in our own strength or understanding. We must have the mind and might of Christ.

So many in the body of Christ live in a terrible state of confusion and difficulty simply because they do not take every thought captive and line up their thinking with the Word of God. Paul strongly admonishes us in his second letter to the Corinthians:

> For though we walk in the flesh, we do not war after the flesh:
>
> (For the weapons of our warfare are not carnal, but mighty through God to the pulling down of strong holds;)
>
> Casting down imaginations, and every high thing that exalteth itself against the knowledge of God, and bringing into captivity every thought to the obedience of Christ.
>
> 2 CORINTHIANS 10:3-5

Christians are having nervous breakdowns, stress attacks, and losing their minds because Satan sends demons to attack them in their thought life and they do not cast down those imaginations that are against God and His Word. Husbands are leaving their wives, and they don't know why. They just say, "I got to go. I still love you. It's not that I don't love you. I'll send you money. No, it's not another woman, I just got to go."

"Well, what's sending you?"

"I don't know. I got to go."

In another home, a woman has fallen in love with somebody else's husband and she's out of control. She doesn't even know why she loves him. He's not somebody she would be attracted to. She doesn't like anybody that looks like him! But she thinks about him so much she's dreaming about him.

Evil spirits are planting thoughts in our minds that are not our thoughts, and we must cast them down. For example, today with the shootings in schools and in churches, many parents are very frightened for their children. This is just what the devil wants! He wants us to be tormented and fearful because then our faith is made completely ineffective. We are now the ones who are hiding in corners just trying to survive when we should be out messing up every tactic of the enemy.

When we send our children off to school and suddenly our heart jumps into our throat because a picture of them being gunned down races through our mind — that is demonic and we must immediately submit our minds to God's Word and drive that mental image out with "my children are taught of the Lord and great is their peace and undisturbed composure. I plead the blood of Jesus over my children, and Satan, you have no right to hurt them or harm them in any way. I take authority over you through the name and the blood of Jesus Christ and declare any strategies or attacks you have planned for my children are made null and void this day and forever!" And we do battle in the spirit until the

Holy Spirit floods our hearts again with the peace that passes all understanding.

If we think any thought that is contrary to what God says in His Word — no matter how pleasant it is — we must put it down also. In most cases, the devil will introduce a thought pattern that is not terrifying, but very comfortable and pleasing, something that strokes our flesh and makes our ego tingle with excitement. But we must fight as hard as we fought for our children! We must submit ourselves immediately to God and His Word, resist the devil, and cause him to flee! (See James 4:7.) It's a fight to hold our homes together and resist the warm fantasy of an affair. It's a fight to finish our assignments and not go to the movies instead. It's a fight to walk in love toward people and make war against evil spirits instead of satisfying our flesh by seeking revenge. And sometimes it's a fight just to get out of bed in the morning!

Our fight is in the supernatural realm, but the Church has become so worldly that the minute someone has a problem, we automatically respond, "They need counseling." We want to sit down and use our human understanding to solve problems that are spiritual. Oftentimes we judge the person who is oppressed. We think we are so smart! The fact is, we are totally ignorant of the reality of spiritual matters and walk in the futility of our intellect. Many of those with problems need *deliverance from* them, not *counseling about* them. Others need to learn how to fight spiritual battles and win them. Still others need to be encouraged in their spiritual battle to stand strong until the victory comes.

Just a generation ago, there were those in the Church who didn't "counsel" anybody. They put a person on the altar! They would plead the blood of Jesus over that person and begin calling on His name. They didn't know much Greek or Hebrew, and they hadn't studied theology or church history, but they would call on His name and plead the blood. And when they did, the power of God would break through in that person's life and freedom would burst forth! They knew who their real enemy was, so oppressive evil was set to flight and lives were changed. Our fathers and mothers of the faith knew how to wrestle the enemy to the ground *in the spiritual realm.*

The revelation the Holy Spirit wants to give us in these verses of Scripture is that we are fighting a very organized and intelligent horde of evil beings. They have studied humans for thousands of years. They worked on our fathers and mothers, our grandfathers and grandmothers, all the way back to Adam and Eve. They know every weakness, every

strength, and how to turn them all against us. But
God has given us a powerful and mighty redemption from this evil! Our hope and assurance of victory is to walk this earth in Christ, stay suited up in the armor of God, and refuse to back down from what God has promised in His Word.

DON'T QUIT!

Wherefore take unto you the whole armour of God, that ye may be able to withstand in the evil day, and having done all, to stand.

EPHESIANS 6:13

Paul says, "Wherefore," or because you are fighting spiritual wickedness, you are to "take unto you the whole armour of God." The Greek language used for "take unto you" gives us great insight into the seriousness of Paul's admonition. "Take unto you" is like a military command that is to be obeyed immediately and for all time. You are to put on God's armor right now and never even consider taking it off. You are to maintain discipline over your flesh and keep your spirit alert so that the Holy Spirit can keep you appraised of the enemy's movements at all times.

When we persevere in the Spirit and keep the armor of God on at all times, we will "be able to withstand in the evil day." I have underlined that word "day" in my Bible because that says to me that the devil's attack is only for a day! He has a limit. He won't last if we'll put on our armor and fight. If we'll stand, his attack will soon be over and he'll have to flee.

Two of the greatest wiles of the devil are *discouragement* and *exhaustion.* If all else fails, he will simply come at us again and again and again to wear us down and get us to quit. When Jesus was in the wilderness and Satan tempted Him, He stood against the devil with the Word of God until the devil simply couldn't stay any longer. The Bible says, "Then the devil leaveth him" (Matthew 4:11). His time was up. Jesus outlasted him and he had to go.

Today, we don't see Joshua and the children of Israel still circling the wall of Jericho! No! They had a certain number of times and then their shout of victory brought the wall to the ground. So be encouraged! The evil coming against you only has a "day"! If you keep standing, his day will soon be over. Whatever is coming against you in the spirit realm isn't permanent. It isn't going to last that long — not if you'll keep God's armor on and stand. Maybe the sun is already setting, the day is nearly over, and evil is about to flee into the night. Paul wrote to the Galatians,

And let us not be weary in well doing: for in due season we shall reap, if we faint not.

GALATIANS 6:9

How many believers have not possessed the promises and blessings of God purely because they got tired of the struggle and quit just moments before all was theirs? How many were inches away from conquering their land and they dropped their sword or their shield to the ground? That thought makes my entire being shudder! What would have happened if Joshua had quit before the seventh time around the walls of Jericho? What would have happened if he gave up before the shout?

Oh God, help us to stop running in our own strength and be endued with Yours, to listen to the voice of our Captain and follow His battle plan, to keep Your armor on at all times, and when we've done all, to continue resisting the discouraging wiles of the devil until the victory is manifested.

When we know our enemy, understand his tactics, stay suited in the whole armor of God, and refuse to budge from His perfect will for our lives, we can defeat the enemy and keep him defeated. We can love people, hate evil, and stay focused on the prize until it is ours.

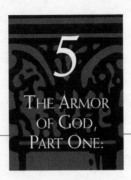

5

THE ARMOR OF GOD, PART ONE:

TRUTH, RIGHTEOUSNESS, AND PEACE

The main thing to remember about the armor of God is that it's *God's* armor. You can't go out to the department store and put on this armor. You cannot think about His armor or imagine yourself in His armor to put it on. You have to move from the outer court of praise into the Holy of Holies of worship and completely surrender to God in order to put on His armor. This is holy armor!

> **S**tand therefore, having your loins girt about with truth, and having on the breastplate of righteousness;
>
> And your feet shod with the preparation of the gospel of peace;
>
> Above all, taking the shield of faith, wherewith ye shall be able to quench all the fiery darts of the wicked.
>
> And take the helmet of salvation, and the sword of the Spirit, which is the word of God.
>
> EPHESIANS 6:14-17

Every piece of the armor of God pertains to our identity in Christ Jesus. The illustration of external armor reflects the internal reality of being *in Him*. Each piece is a mirror image of a spiritual truth concerning who we are in Christ.

Who is our truth? Jesus Christ!

Who is our righteousness? Jesus Christ!

Who is the one who establishes us in the Gospel of peace? Jesus Christ!

Who is the author and finisher of our faith? Jesus Christ!

Who is our Savior? Jesus Christ!

Who is the living, incarnate Word of God? Jesus Christ!

All of the armor we wear for spiritual battle is found in Christ Jesus!

No doubt the apostle Paul was thinking of the armor of the Roman soldier when he received the revelation of our spiritual armor from the Holy Spirit. From the many times he was imprisoned and heavily guarded by them, Paul spent hours in the company of the Roman guard. He was well familiar with their armor!

This analogy only applies to a certain point, however. The natural armor *covered* a Roman soldier from head to foot, but our spiritual armor permeates and purifies our entire being. The armor of

God fully equips us for the spiritual war we wage in spirit, soul, and body. No matter how big we are on the outside, we are ten feet tall and filled with the glory and power of God on the inside when we suit up in God's armor. Putting on the armor of God makes us holy as He is holy, and it all begins with facing the truth and getting rid of all the lies.

LOINS GIRT ABOUT WITH TRUTH

> **S**tand therefore, having your loins girt about with truth.
>
> EPHESIANS 6:14

Paul begins with a belt or girdle which the Roman soldier wore around his loins. This piece held some of the other pieces of armor in place, including the breastplate, which was attached to it, and the sword, which hung from it. The support and tension around the middle of the soldier's body also served as an attitude check, saying to the soldier, "You're here to fight. You've got a job to do. Keep focused."

The obvious application is that we cannot accomplish anything for the kingdom of God if our lives are not based on truth. In the Greek, this word "truth" does not just refer to God's written Word, but to an honesty of heart and purity of motive. We cannot win a spiritual battle if we are lying to ourselves, deceiving others, and running from the conviction of the Holy Spirit. Our foundation is shifting sand, and we will be tossed to and fro by the wiles of the devil if we do not stand in truth.

Being brutally honest with ourselves is often difficult and many times painful. Ask any woman who wears a girdle or any soldier who has cinched up that belt around his loins — it isn't very comfortable! The belt of truth squeezes us! It causes us to come clean with God and get real about our lives.

Our "loins" also represent our reproductive organs, the most private area of our bodies. When we allow the Holy Spirit to deal with deception and lies in our lives, all our secret places that perhaps no one but our spouses know about are laid bare before Him. These are areas where we are so deceived we don't even know we're deceived. These are areas where we are so ashamed, we are embarrassed that God knows about them. The trouble is, the enemy knows about these secret places too! That's why I believe the Holy Spirit begins with truth. *Truth is the foundation for the entire armor.* If we do not get healed and delivered in these weak areas of our lives, the devil will use them to divert us from God's plan and eventually destroy us.

Since the loins are our reproductive organs, Paul is also saying to the Ephesians, "Don't reproduce anything that is not rooted in truth. Don't reproduce anything that is based upon a lie. Reproduce God's truth." This is a powerful principle of the kingdom of God! Our loins contain the potential of our God-given creativity to reproduce spiritual things that will extend into eternity, things that will have everlasting value and significance! Unfortunately, our loins also have the capability to reproduce a lie.

Many Christians today are reproducing things based on anything but the truth of God's Word. They are reproducing their past. They are acting on the basis of something the Lord has declared null and void long ago. Some are reproducing things based upon what others have said about them. Others are acting on the basis of insufficient information, and in many cases, false information. Still others are reproducing things based upon what they see and know in the temporal, natural realm. They are acting on the basis of information that is not eternal.

We should never engage in the production of anything that rests upon a false premise, but deal only in honesty and truth as we engage in any form of ministry or battle with the enemy. We must speak only God's truth about ourselves, and we must engage only in those activities that are in line with the truth of God, those things which God declares to be holy, pure, and righteous. We must act only as we know Jesus would act because He is literally walking in our shoes by the power of the Holy Spirit in us. *When our loins are girded with truth, we are completely identified in our innermost being with Christ Jesus.*

The enemy will always try to sidetrack us by enticing us to lie and operate according to that lie. Jesus called our enemy the father of all liars and said that no truth was to be found in him. (See John 8:44.) He will try to get us into frustration and restlessness and worry on the basis of lies. He may present the thought that we aren't worthy of God's promises, that we are just not good enough, that our past negates our future, that we can't truly minister in the Lord's name, and he'll say, "What you see is what you're always going to get." Our response to these lies is to declare what *God* says about us — now and forever!

The devil may also use another, more deadly tactic on us. He will reinforce our comfort with sin. He will say things like, "The grace of God is so great, go ahead and sin for a little while. He'll forgive you later. Look at that magazine. Take a drink. Smoke that joint. Fantasize about another man's wife. Have an affair. The IRS won't miss that amount. Just take the dress. God knows you need it and you don't have the money." The moment the snake introduces these evil thoughts and desires, we must jerk ourselves up on our most holy faith and declare the truth! "Devil, my trust and comfort are in God and God alone, so get out of my life!"

Any involvement in *lying* also endangers us. Speaking a lie destroys trust, a vital component in our relationships. When we lie about someone else, we disrupt our relationship with that person, other people's relationships with that person, and our relationship with God. When lying occurs frequently in a body of believers, eventually no one trusts anyone else, and some will not even trust God.

Believing and acting upon a lie of the devil is a terrible experience, but it doesn't necessarily mean we don't trust God. We may be honestly deceived. However, deliberately lying about something or someone is simply not trusting God to work all things for our good. We step in to cover our tracks and clean up the mess ourselves, but in the end we make a bigger mess than we started with. So it always pays to tell the truth and to be totally honest with God, with ourselves, and with others.

When you are girded with truth, you are planted squarely on the rock of Jesus Christ and every other piece of armor can be securely fastened onto you. But don't even think about putting on the breastplate of righteousness or the sword of the Spirit if you aren't girded with truth!

THE BREASTPLATE OF RIGHTEOUSNESS

*...**a**nd having on the breastplate of righteousness.*

EPHESIANS 6:14

The Roman soldier's breastplate covered everything from his shoulders to his loins, and its main purpose was to protect him from a life-threatening wound to the heart. In God's armor, righteousness deals with the essence of our spiritual condition in Christ, keeping our hearts pure and open to God. Although we hear and use the term "righteousness" frequently in the Church, do we really know what it means?

Righteousness originates in God alone. It is His standard of motive, behavior, and character. God embodies righteousness because everything He says and does is absolutely, eternally *right*. When the Word of God declares that we are righteous through the blood of Jesus, we are absolutely, eternally right with God. Moreover, we are like God in our spirit. The Bible tells us that through Adam we were made sinners, but through Jesus Christ we are *made* righteous:

> **F**or as by one man's disobedience many were made sinners, so by the obedience of one shall many be made righteous.

ROMANS 5:19

Notice that we were *made* righteous, not *covered* with righteousness. In the Old Testament, the blood sacrifices covered believers. God demonstrated this first when He killed animals and used their skins to cover Adam and Eve's nakedness after they had sinned. But in the New Testament, Jesus Christ made the absolute, eternal blood sacrifice so that believers could *be* righteous. The Greek word used for "made" is *katastatheesontai,* which indicates a permanent condition of *being.*

The Word of God says that we become the righteousness of God the moment we believe in Jesus Christ and are saved. Afterward, when we put on the breastplate of righteousness as believers, we are literally allowing the righteousness of God to manifest in our lives. We are coming to grips with our identity as children of God, made in His image. We are not to take His righteousness and cover our sinful nature because we now have God's nature in our hearts. We are simply choosing to live from God's nature and righteousness instead of our own.

We must never count on our own righteousness! The Bible declares that our righteousness is as filthy rags before the Father:

> **B**ut we are all as an unclean thing, and all our righteousnesses are as filthy rags; and we all do fade

as a leaf; and our iniquities, like the wind, have taken us away.

ISAIAH 64:6

This verse means we are never justified in saying, "I am righteous because I have lived a good life. After all, I've fasted for twenty-two days and thirty-six minutes, so this promise should be mine. My grandfather was a Christian and my father was a Christian and I'm a Christian, so there's great reward coming to our family. I'm a good person. I go to church and sing in the choir. I give to the poor all the time!"

No! Our righteousness must rest only in the shed blood of Jesus Christ, which transforms our lives from the inside out and wraps us up in His identity. Then our only legitimate declaration to the enemy is not what we have made of ourselves, but what Jesus has made us to be in Him. The truth is, we have no power over the enemy and even place ourselves in his hands when we stand in our own goodness.

When we start declaring our self-righteousness to the devil, we place ourselves in great jeopardy because it is impossible to withstand the attacks of the enemy in our own goodness. We open up ourselves to the devil's scorn, and he's going to laugh in our faces. He's going to say, "And who are you?"

Remember the seven sons of a man named Sceva?
They didn't possess the righteousness of Jesus
Christ, and they attempted to cast out an evil spirit
in Jesus' name. The evil spirit responded, "Jesus I
know, and Paul I know; but who are ye?" (Acts
19:15). As a result, the "man in whom the evil spirit
was leaped on them, and overcame them, and
prevailed against them, so that they fled out of that
house naked and wounded" (Acts 19:16). It's not a
good idea to stand in your own righteousness!

Our righteousness does not stand in anything we
have done, are doing, or will ever do. No person can
earn righteousness or attain it on their own merits.
Our righteousness exists solely because we are in
relationship with the only Righteous One who ever
walked this earth. Paul wrote to the Philippians,

> **A**nd be found in him, not having mine own right-
> eousness, which is of the law, but that which is through
> the faith of Christ, the righteousness which is of God
> by faith.
>
> PHILIPPIANS 3:9

When we put on the breastplate of righteousness
and identify fully with Jesus Christ, we purge
ourselves of sin, make our flesh come in line, and
put off the old man. We allow God's righteousness
to come forth in our motives, our thoughts, and our
deeds. Then we are in a position to bear spiritual

fruit, to discern and display all things that are excellent, and we are called "sincere and without offence till the day of Christ" (Philippians 1:10). Paul wrote to the Philippians:

> **B**eing filled with the fruits of righteousness, which are by Jesus Christ, unto the glory and praise of God.
>
> PHILIPPIANS 1:11

The righteousness of Jesus Christ puts us in the spiritual position to choose the right things, do the right things, say the right things, and stand holy and spotless before the enemy. Confronted with the righteousness of God, the devil must flee from us! He cannot wound our hearts because God's breastplate of righteousness is in place. All he sees is the bride of Christ, and the Bible tells us how we are clothed:

> **L**et us be glad and rejoice, and give honour to him: for the marriage of the Lamb is come, and his wife hath made herself ready.
> And to her was granted that she should be arrayed in fine linen, clean and white: for the fine linen is the righteousness of saints.
>
> REVELATION 19:7-8

Putting on the breastplate of righteousness purifies and protects our hearts and centers our lives on God. When we meditate on and wonder at the awesome reality that we are righteous through Jesus' blood, that the Father looks at us and sees a pure, shining-bright saint and not the terrible sinner we have been, all we want to do is that which is right in God's eyes! None of the devil's temptations hold any allure for us. None of his lies entice us because all we want is God. A purified heart is a protected heart and a strong heart. None of the tactics of the devil will prevail when our hearts beat with the righteousness of God through Jesus Christ our Lord!

THE GOSPEL OF PEACE

And your feet shod with the preparation of the gospel of peace.

EPHESIANS 6:15

Paul tells us to put on the armor of God so we can stand against evil, but how can we stand if our feet are injured or not working properly? Remember Mephibosheth, Jonathan's son and King Saul's grandson? He was dropped on his feet as a small child. As a result, he was lame in both feet and had to be carried everywhere he went. (See 2 Samuel 4:4.) This is not a picture of standing strong!

Physically, our feet provide balance to our entire body and are a major component of our ability to move from one place to another. When our feet are injured our whole body is affected. Although our feet are precious parts of our body, they are often neglected and overlooked until something happens to them.

It is so important to protect our feet from harm, which is why wearing the proper shoes is vital. Though shoes are now seen as fashion statements, they really function to protect our feet from injuries that would impair our walking or even prohibit us from walking altogether. For the soldier, however, having the proper shoes can mean the difference between life and death, victory and defeat.

The Roman soldier wore a very distinctive shoe in battle. The *caliga*, a strong, sandal-type shoe, had a sole studded with nails which pierced the ground and provided tremendous stability. To add to this illustration, Paul uses the word *hetoimazo*, which the *King James Version* translates "preparation," but would best be translated "established" or "a firm foundation." As the *caliga* provided a firm foundation for the Roman soldier, we are established and have a firm foundation in the Gospel of peace.

Next, we need to distinguish the phrase, "gospel of peace," from the phrase, "the Gospel." Paul is not talking specifically about spreading the Gospel; but rather, he is pointing out one of the benefits of the Gospel: the peace of God. The Gospel settles, strengthens, and stabilizes believers.

Then we have the word "shod," which is one of those antiquated words simply meaning to cover our feet. However, the word used in the context of this verse has a greater meaning, "to put under or bind under." The thought is that our feet should never touch the ground in their bare form. We should walk on the protective, peaceful cushion of the Gospel.

Ephesians 6:15 is saying that *the firm foundation of the Gospel is that we walk in peace.*

- We have peace with God through our Lord Jesus Christ. (See Romans 5:1.)
- We have peace between Jew and Gentile (see Ephesians 2:14) as well as among races, social and economic classes, and genders. (See Galatians 3:28.)
- We have peace in believing, which causes us to abound in hope. (See Romans 15:13.)
- We have peace in the Holy Spirit. (See Galatians 5:22.)
- We are unified as a body through the bond of peace. (See Ephesians 4:3.)
- We have peace from God at all times. (See 2 Thessalonians 3:16.)

The Bible also says that we are not to go anywhere or do anything, think any thought or make any statement, which does not maintain the peace of God in our lives. Only the peace of God will keep us standing firm when the violent attacks of the enemy come against us.

> **F**or ye shall go out with joy, and be led forth with peace.
>
> ISAIAH 55:12

> **A**nd let the peace of God rule in your hearts.
>
> COLOSSIANS 3:15

> **A**nd make straight paths for your feet....
> Follow peace with all men.
>
> HEBREWS 12:13-14

> **A**nd the peace of God, which passeth all understanding, shall keep your hearts and minds through Christ Jesus.
>
> PHILIPPIANS 4:7

Not only do feet support the entire body, but they take us wherever we go. Thus, the feet represent our will. When our feet are shod with the Gospel of peace, we will go only where God gives us peace to go. We will not obey any other voice but His because only His voice gives us peace. The peace of God brings balance to our lives, keeps our priorities in godly order, and shows us His perfect will. *God's peace is our compass in life.*

When the devil does his utmost to get us to walk down this wrong path and that wrong path, to lead us astray, the peace of God will keep us on the right road. The enemy will introduce false teachings and false doctrines to capture our minds. He will present alluring and seductive temptations, trying to get us to take idols into our hearts. But when we wear our gospel shoes of peace, we will believe only God's Word, walk only where the Holy Spirit gives us peace to walk, and worship only Jesus! Any lack of peace will alert us that we are off the path and headed for the devil's quicksand, and God's peace will lead us back to the safety of His will.

Spiritually then, having our feet fitted with or bound with the Gospel of peace keeps our will firmly established in God's will and our walk with Jesus unhindered. Our hearts and minds are led by peace and we have no need to fear the enemy. Therefore, we should put on the firm foundation of the Gospel of peace at all times.

Stay in alignment with God's commandments to you. Walk out the prophecy He has spoken over your life. Direct your path toward those things that the Holy Spirit says belong to you. Read in Habakkuk,

> **W**rite the vision, and make it plain upon tables, that he may run that readeth it.
>
> HABAKKUK 2:2

I love to teach, "Write it, read it, and run it." Whatever God has told you He will do in your life, write it down. Refer to it often, and live as if you are already receiving it. Don't go into places or situations where the name of Jesus isn't lifted up. Don't get your feet tangled up in relationships that conflict with God's will for your life. Don't get bogged down in projects and ideas that fail to bring glory to God. Go only where the Gospel is welcome and the peace of the Lord prevails.

You begin to put on the armor of God by first baring your soul to Him in complete honesty and truth, making certain that your mind and heart are totally in line with His Word. When this belt of truth is firmly in place around the most private areas of your life, then you can attach the breast-plate of righteousness, which declares that you stand absolutely and eternally right before God through the blood of Jesus Christ. Next, you put on your gospel shoes of God's peace and line up your will and your way with God's will.

At this point you have purified your heart, embraced the reality of who you are in Christ, and faced the right direction. You are ready to put on the rest of God's armor.

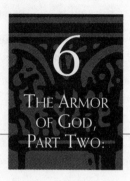

6

THE ARMOR OF GOD, PART TWO:

FAITH, SALVATION, AND GOD'S WORD

THE SHIELD OF FAITH

Above all, taking the shield of faith, wherewith ye shall be able to quench all the fiery darts of the wicked.

EPHESIANS 6:16

We must first address the phrase, "Above all," because it adds a lot of depth to our understanding of faith as spiritual armor. The Greek language could be translated, "In addition to," in which case Paul would be saying, "Not only do you need the belt of truth, the breastplate of righteousness, and the gospel shoes of peace, but you also need the shield of faith." But this phrase could also be translated, "Over all," in which case Paul is saying, "Covering and protecting all the pieces of God's armor is the shield of faith." Either way you look at it, Paul is emphasizing the importance of faith in spiritual warfare.

The writer of Hebrews says it is impossible to please God without faith.

> **B**ut without faith it is impossible to please him: for he that cometh to God must believe that he is, and that he is a rewarder of them that diligently seek him.
>
> HEBREWS 11:6

Furthermore, if we ever doubt the vital significance of faith, all we need to do is research how often Jesus talked about it. He commended people for their faith and even marveled at the centurion's faith:

> **W**hen Jesus heard it, he marvelled, and said to them that followed, Verily I say unto you, I have not found so great faith, no, not in Israel.
>
> MATTHEW 8:10

Jesus also marveled at unbelief, however. He appeared disappointed and even exasperated when people had no faith, such as when His disciples had no faith during a storm:

> **A**nd he arose, and rebuked the wind, and said unto the sea, Peace, be still. And the wind ceased, and there was a great calm.
>
> And he said unto them, Why are ye so fearful? how is it that ye have no faith?
>
> MARK 4:39-40

Jesus told many who were healed that they were healed because of their faith:

> **A**nd he said unto her, Daughter, be of good comfort: thy faith hath made thee whole; go in peace.
>
> LUKE 8:48

The Bible even says that Jesus himself could not do many miracles in His hometown because the people lacked faith:

> **A**nd he did not many mighty works there because of their unbelief.
>
> MATTHEW 13:58

The shield of faith, therefore, is a part of God's armor that we need to study well!

> **A**bove all, taking the shield of faith, wherewith ye shall be able to quench all the fiery darts of the wicked.
>
> EPHESIANS 6:16

The Greek word translated "shield" tells us a lot because there were two kinds of shields in Paul's time. This word is *thureos*, which refers to the Roman soldier's *scutum*, the larger shield which was the size of a door. It was big, well constructed, and fully protected the warrior in battle. This shield was the first piece of armor that came in contact with the enemy, so it had to be strong and formidable.

When the enemy attacks, our faith will meet him and defeat him!

In Paul's day, soldiers often dipped their arrows into combustible fluids and lit them so that their arrows would burn whatever they hit. No doubt, these "fire arrows" were what Paul was referring to when he mentioned the "fiery darts of the wicked." When soldiers saw that the enemy was using fiery darts, they immediately prepared their shields, which were made of an iron frame covered with layers of leather. They would soak their shields in water so that when a fiery dart hit, it would fizzle out in a puff of smoke.

With what are we to soak our shields? Throughout Scripture, water is a symbol for the Word of God:

> *That he might sanctify and cleanse it with the washing of water by the word.*

> EPHESIANS 5:26

Paul says that our faith grows, matures, and gains strength by reading, studying, meditating upon, and living by the Word of God:

> *So then faith cometh by hearing, and hearing by the word of God.*

> ROMANS 10:17

To win the victory in spiritual warfare, you must soak your mind with the Word of God. Your faith in God's Word and *knowing* God's Word, that unshakable confidence and trust in the reliability of what God says, will quench every fiery dart of the enemy. The more you read the Word of God, the more you will think the Word, feel the Word, and respond with the Word. The more your faith grows, the more your life will reflect the Word, be grounded in the Word, and be in complete alignment with the Word.

Whatever the enemy shoots your way isn't going to sting if you know the Word because your faith and trust will be entirely in Jesus, the Living Word. You will have no fear of what the devil and his demons will do to you because you will be walking hand-in-hand and arm-in-arm with the King of Kings and Lord of Lords.

The fiery dart will hit your shield with, "Your children are never going to serve God!" Your shield will quench it with, "Isaiah 54:13 says that my children are taught of the Lord and great is their peace in Him."

The fiery dart will hit your shield with, "You're going crazy! The stress of all your problems is too much for you. You'll never make it!" Your shield will quench it with, "Philippians 4:13 says that I can do all things through Christ who strengthens me!"

The fiery dart will hit your shield with, "Flu season is coming! Get ready to be sick!" Your shield will quench it with, "2 Peter 2:24 and Isaiah 53:5 declare that by the stripes of Jesus Christ, I am healed!"

The fiery dart will hit your shield with, "Look around you. This world is out of control with earthquakes, hurricanes, tornadoes, and volcanic eruptions! Planes are crashing and trains are derailing and gangs are shooting people in the streets!" Your shield will quench it with, "Read Psalm 91, Devil! Read 2 Timothy 1:7! I dwell in the secret place of the Most High and fear nothing because I have the love of God, the power of the Holy Spirit, and the mind of Christ!"

Paul did not say that knowing the Word would keep the devil from shooting fiery darts at you! What he said was that *when* the devil shoots his arrows, the Word of God that is in you will protect you. The fiery darts won't break your heart or penetrate your soul. They won't cause a firestorm of worry, frustration, depression, or anxiety in your life.

> **N**o *weapon that is formed against thee shall prosper; and every tongue that shall rise against thee in judgment thou shalt condemn. This is the heritage of the servants of the Lord, and their righteousness is of me, saith the Lord.*
>
> ISAIAH 54:17

Rumors, innuendoes, and false reports may be fired against you, but they won't hurt your heart if you have your faith saturated with God's Word. The devil may come at you with all kinds of threats, accusations, and lies, but they won't lodge in your spirit and burn there if you have your faith saturated with God's Word. Satan may tempt you with worldly riches and honor and power, but the Word of God in you will give you the strength to resist and the devil will flee!

The shield of faith meets the attack of the enemy with God's Word, and our unswerving trust in our God makes it impossible for the devil to prevail.

THE HELMET OF SALVATION

And take the helmet of salvation....

EPHESIANS 6:17

Some parts of the Roman soldier's armor were elaborate and expensive because they were designed to make a statement of indomitable strength and authority. Other than the large shield, the helmet made the biggest impression. It covered the head entirely, including cheek pieces; and it was made of bronze, with ornate carvings and etchings. To help the soldier bear the weight of the helmet, it was lined with a soft, spongy material.

The helmet was extremely heavy, and only the sharpest ax or heaviest hammer could pierce it.

Without this kind of protection, the soldier would quickly lose his head! But the helmet also had the most flamboyant feature in the entire armor of God: a tall plume on the top made of feathers or horsehair. This plume was extremely striking and made the soldier look as much as two feet taller than he actually was.

By calling this piece of spiritual armor "the helmet of salvation," Paul could not have made a more powerful statement about our redemption. When we truly understand and appreciate that we are eternally, perfectly, and absolutely saved, that we are forgiven and cleansed through the blood of Jesus Christ, and that we are completely reconciled to God, we stand ten feet tall!

When we know we are God's child and walk in His presence, people notice our confidence and strength. They sense a courage and strength about us. Furthermore, when everyone around us is "losing their heads" because of the stresses and strains of life, we keep ours because of the joy of our salvation!

Because the helmet of salvation covers the head, Paul is saying that our minds must be stayed at all times upon the most basic of all spiritual truths: We are saved! We must keep this reality at the forefront of our thinking always. So many Christians today spend the bulk of their praise time rejoicing over the fact that the Lord has given them power and authority. They are thanking God for this gift and that healing and another person's deliverance. This is good, but Jesus told us specifically that there was only one reason to praise God and rejoice:

> **N**otwithstanding in this rejoice not, that the spirits are subject unto you; but rather rejoice, because your names are written in heaven.
>
> LUKE 10:20

The disciples had just returned from casting out demons and healing the sick all over the country-side, and they were rejoicing at their newfound authority. Jesus pulled them back to center by reminding them that none of this was possible without salvation. *None of the blessings of this life compare to the eternal life we have in Christ Jesus.*

Rejoice that you are saved! You have eternal life! Your sins have been cast as far from you as the east is from the west and the slate of your soul has been wiped clean! You have no reason for guilt, no reason for shame, and you can remind the devil of that fact whenever he tries to bring up the past. No matter what he says to you, just say right back, "Satan, I'm saved and you cannot touch me, deceive me, or defeat me. Jesus Christ died on the cross for me. He shed His blood for me, and when I gave my life to Him my sins were forgiven and I became heavenbound. Nothing can ever change the fact that I am a child of God. I'm saved and I'm going to live forever with Him."

If things look bad today, you are saved!

If things are not turning out as you had thought they would, you are saved!

If you don't yet have all the things you have been promised by God, you are saved!

No matter what others may think about you, say about you, or do to you, you are saved!

Your salvation is the greatest blessing you can ever know and the greatest gift you can ever receive.

Putting on the helmet of salvation means dwelling on your salvation. Meditate on it. Remind yourself of it. The devil cannot upset or distract a mind that is focused on the blessed salvation of Jesus Christ, and the reality of knowing your salvation will make you stand ten feet tall in the Spirit!

THE SWORD OF THE SPIRIT

> ...and the sword of the Spirit, which is the word of God.
>
> EPHESIANS 6:17

Our belt of truth, our breastplate of righteousness, our helmet of salvation, our gospel shoes of peace, and our shield of faith are all defensive armor. But now we must put on the one piece of offensive armor we are given: "the sword of the Spirit, which is the word of God."

When we hear the word "sword," we immediately imagine pirates, Robin Hood, and Zorro wielding long swords that have fancy handles. But the Greek word Paul chose for "sword" in this verse is *machairan*, which refers to a dagger. He chose a large, knife-like weapon over the heavy broadsword (the one Robin Hood used) and the lighter foil-like version (the one Zorro used). By using *machairan*, Paul indicates that we fight spiritual battles at close range.

> **F**or the word of God is quick, and powerful, and sharper than any two-edged sword, piercing even to the dividing asunder of soul and spirit, and of the joints and marrow, and is a discerner of the thoughts and intents of the heart.
>
> HEBREWS 4:12

This verse in Hebrews provides even more information about the *machairan*. The word "quick" is the Greek word *zoon*, which means "life." The Word of God is alive, powerful, and sharp. It has pinpoint accuracy to determine exactly what is going on in our lives. When we enter into spiritual warfare, we come nose to nose with the devil and every wickedness of this world's system. So it is imperative that we have a weapon that is capable of rendering the enemy powerless. Because Jesus is our Captain, let's see how He dealt with Satan.

Then was Jesus led up of the Spirit into the wilderness to be tempted of the devil.

And when he had fasted forty days and forty nights, he was afterward an hungered.

And when the tempter came to him, he said, If thou be the Son of God, command that these stones be made bread.

But he answered and said, It is written, Man shall not live by bread alone, but by every word that proceedeth out of the mouth of God.

Then the devil taketh him up into the holy city, and setteth him on a pinnacle of the temple,

And saith unto him, If thou be the Son of God, cast thyself down: for it is written, He shall give his angels charge concerning thee: and in their hands they shall bear thee up, lest at any time thou dash thy foot against a stone.

Jesus said unto him, It is written again, Thou shalt not tempt the Lord thy God.

Again, the devil taketh him up into an exceeding high mountain, and sheweth him all the kingdoms of the world, and the glory of them;

And saith unto him, All these things will I give thee, if thou wilt fall down and worship me.

Then saith Jesus unto him, Get thee hence, Satan: for it is written, Thou shalt worship the Lord thy God, and him only shalt thou serve.

Then the devil leaveth him, and, behold, angels came and ministered unto him.

MATTHEW 4:1-11

Three times the devil came to Jesus with powerful temptations, and three times the only weapon Jesus used to fight him was the Word of God. Again and again, He said, "It is written," and Satan finally had to give up and leave Him alone.

To wield the Word of God in battle, however, we have to *know* the Word of God. We cannot just memorize it and give it mental ascent. We have to have it hidden deep in our hearts. The only way for that to happen is to read it, study it, hear it — and keep reading, studying, and hearing it until we *know* it — for example, until we know that we are the righteousness of God through Christ Jesus as well as we know our name.

The Word of God must be "quick" or alive in your mind and heart, and then it will be "powerful" when you speak it in a time of crisis or battle. God's Word should be your automatic response to every challenge of life.

If the situation incites praise and thanksgiving, then a word of thanksgiving and praise should come alive in your mind and heart and then flow in power from your lips.

If the situation demands confrontation in the spirit, then a word of rebuke or deliverance should come alive in your mind and heart and then flow in power from your lips.

If the situation is rooted in falsehood or guilt or shame or lies, then a word of truth should come alive in your mind and heart and then flow in power from your lips.

If you really want to do damage to the enemy in the spirit realm, declare the Word of God to him from your heart! He may hang around for awhile to see if you really mean it, if the Word really is alive in you; but if it is, eventually this dead, corrupt evil spirit won't be able to endure being continually stabbed and cut with the very life of God, and he will flee!

Now you are completely fitted in God's magnificent armor. You have washed yourself in truth, identified with Christ in righteousness, established your will in God's peace, placed your faith and trust only in Him, raised your spiritual stature by focusing on your awesome salvation, and gripped the Word of God in your heart and mind. The time has come for you to take the Promised Land!

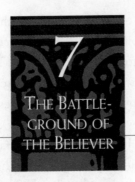

7

THE BATTLE-GROUND OF THE BELIEVER

As we put on the whole armor of God and after we are fully prepared and equipped for battle, the apostle Paul says, "Pray!"

Praying always with all prayer and supplication in the Spirit....

EPHESIANS 6:18

Prayer is the battleground of the believer.

A powerless, gutless, ineffective Church is a prayerless Church.

When the Church doesn't pray, we are not even on the battleground. We take nothing back from the enemy, we have no effect for the kingdom of God, and most likely, we are being trampled by sin and the oppression of wicked spirits. When the Church doesn't pray, we are giving the enemy an open door to steal, kill, and destroy us. On the other hand, if we pray, we become Jesus' warrior bride!

What do you think Joshua and the children of Israel were doing when they marched seven times around the great wall of Jericho? They weren't talking politics. They weren't reminiscing about the past. They weren't discussing the latest blockbuster movie. They weren't even conferring about Church doctrine. No! I believe they were praying, silently communing with the God of their fathers.

The great wall of Jericho fell down flat by the power of God that was released through the prayer and obedience of Joshua and the children of Israel.

The Lord commands us to pray and then obey so that He can do great exploits! We spent the first few chapters of this book discussing the absolute necessity for obedience when it comes to waging a successful war. But now the apostle Paul reveals the other side to this coin: *We have nothing to obey if we do not pray!*

God commands us to pray, authorizes us to pray, and He says that He cannot act in many situations unless we pray. Yet believers will do anything to avoid praying. We would rather jump up and down in wild praises to the Lord than stay in our prayer closet and pray. In fact, I believe the Church must accomplish in prayer what we have accomplished in praise and worship. We have praise singers and praise dancers and praise banners and praise trumpets.

We have all kinds of praise, everything from country to classical in style. We know all of the Hebrew words for praise. There has been tremendous teaching on praise and worship. But how many of us are prayer warriors?

How many of us spend time on our faces before God and petition Him daily?

How many of us consider the highlight of our existence to be those times spent in powerful prayer, basking in the warmth of God's presence and receiving revelation?

How many of us travail before the Lord in the Spirit until deliverance breaks forth and people are set free from the grip of the enemy?

How many of us refuse to take the devil's bondage and persist in prayer until the devil desists?

It was because Joshua tarried in the tabernacle that he took the Promised Land!

ALWAYS MEANS *ALWAYS!*

Praying always....

EPHESIANS 6:18

The Greek word for "Praying" indicates that this is not just bringing our requests and petitions, but it also means worship. We are not just to speak, but we are also to listen. And the word "always" tells us not only to have an attitude of prayer at all times, but to take every opportunity to pray — for ourselves, for our loved ones, and for anyone else who crosses our path.

Johnny comes in crying because he skinned his knee — let's pray!

The rent is due tomorrow and the money is not in the bank — let's pray!

A crisis happens at work and important decisions need to be made — let's pray!

Next-door neighbor's child has run away from home — let's pray!

Paul repeats the command to pray in 1 Thessalonians 5:17 as "Pray without ceasing." Prayer is something the Lord expects us to engage in constantly, which means prayer must be something we *can* do at all times and in all situations. This is possible because there are different types of prayer, even silent prayer, which is communing in our hearts with God. If we are in a place where we cannot speak, we can still commune in our hearts with God. When we stay in an attitude of prayer, nothing can separate us from Him and we can remain in communication with Him always.

Prayer is vital to spiritual warfare because we must commune with God to put on His armor. We must communicate with Him to receive His battle plan, and sometimes He tells us of battles to come.

Then we can allow Him to prepare us. As a result of maintaining an attitude of prayer, whenever and however the enemy strikes, we are suited up for warfare and ready to fight and win. Although we do not live in a constant state of warfare, we do live in a constant attitude of prayer because the enemy is roaming the earth, seeking whom he may devour:

> **B**e sober, be vigilant; because your adversary the devil, as a roaring lion, walketh about, seeking whom he may devour.
>
> 1 PETER 5:8

I cannot emphasize this enough: Prayer connects us to God, and God knows the strategies and battle plans that will defeat the enemy. David said of the Lord, "He teacheth my hands to war" (Psalm 18:34). In other words, "The Lord has taught me how to fight the battles I face. He gives me the victory." We must rely fully on the Lord as David relied upon Him:

> **I**t is God that girdeth me with strength, and maketh my way perfect.
>
> He maketh my feet like hinds' feet, and setteth me upon my high places.
>
> He teacheth my hands to war, so that a bow of steel is broken by mine arms.
>
> Thou hast also given me the shield of thy salvation: and thy right hand hath holden me up, and thy gentleness hath made me great.

Thou has enlarged my steps under me, that my feet did not slip.

I have pursued mine enemies, and overtaken them: neither did I turn again till they were consumed.

I have wounded them that they were not able to rise: they are fallen under my feet.

For thou hast girded me with strength unto the battle: thou hast subdued under me those that rose up against me.

Thou hast also given me the necks of mine enemies, that I might destroy them that hate me.

PSALM 18:32-40

David was a man after God's own heart and one of the most unusual believers of the Old Testament. He was a man of war who recognized that the only way to defeat the enemy in the natural was to defeat the enemy in the spirit realm first. He knew that prayer was the real battleground for all the issues of life. Throughout his lifetime, whether he was a shepherd, a hero, a fugitive, or a king, David trusted the Lord for his safety and his provision from day to day, week to week, month to month, and year to year — communing continually with the Lord in prayer.

ALL PRAYER AND SUPPLICATION

Praying always with all prayer and supplication in the Spirit, and watching thereunto with all perseverance and supplication for all saints;

And for me, that utterance may be given unto me,
that I may open my mouth boldly, to make known the
mystery of the gospel,

For which I am an ambassador in bonds: that
therein I may speak boldly, as I ought to speak.

EPHESIANS 6:18-20

Paul initially calls upon the Ephesians to pray for him that he will be even more bold in making known the mystery of the Gospel. Paul, perhaps the boldest preacher in the history of the Church, asks for prayer that he can be even more bold! This statement always puts me to shame! Am I praying such a prayer today? Am I asking that believers everywhere, especially myself, might be even more bold in declaring the Gospel to an unbelieving world?

It's time to pray until we tear down the strongholds of the enemy that are being built against our personal lives, our families, our churches, and the body of Christ in this generation — so we can preach the Gospel boldly. It's time we pray until those who are being persecuted for the Gospel's sake around the world are set free to continue preaching boldly. It's time we pray for missionaries who are getting souls saved in those remote, easy-to-forget areas of the world, that they may be even more bold.

Paul also exhorts us to pray "with all prayer and supplication for all saints." He says, "Be specific and be thorough. Cover all the bases. Don't leave any stone unturned. Pray about every area of your life and everything that concerns you. Pray about your level of commitment and purity of heart toward the Lord. Pray about your family, your church, your job, and your ministry. Pray about everything the Holy Spirit brings to mind. Oh, and pray for *all the saints* in this way too."

When Paul addresses the Ephesians, he illustrates how thorough we are to be in prayer with his own situation. He doesn't ask the Ephesians to pray for him in only one area. He also makes provision for them to know all his needs so that they might pray more effectively and specifically for his entire life. He writes,

> **B**ut that ye also may know my affairs, and how I do, Tychicus, a beloved brother and faithful minister in the Lord, shall make known to you all things:
> Whom I have sent unto you for the same purpose, that ye might know our affairs, and that he might comfort your hearts.

EPHESIANS 6:21-22

When we pray for each other, we are to pray with the most accurate information we can obtain. When was the last time you prayed about something until you knew in your heart and mind that you had prayed about every facet of that problem

114

or situation? So often we pray, "Oh, Lord, You
know the need. Please meet the need." But the Bible
says that we are to pray with wisdom and understanding. We are to pray about everything we know
to pray. We are to pray about a problem inside and
out, upside and down, through and through.

Pray thoroughly. Pray all the way through a
problem. Pray every aspect and every detail and
every consequence of a situation. And pray for the
entire body of Christ to prosper in all areas of life.
This sounds like a lot to do! However, Paul also
gives us the key to doing it.

WATCHING, PERSEVERING PRAYER

*Praying always with all prayer and supplication
in the Spirit, and watching thereunto with all perseverance and supplication for all saints.*

EPHESIANS 6:18

We are to pray "watching thereunto with all
perseverance." The Greek word translated "watching" is *agrupneo*, which means to be sleepless, to be
always awake and alert. And "perseverance" is the
word *proskartereo*, which means to give constant care
and attention. Not only are we to pray for ourselves,
for all the saints, and for all the ministers of the
Gospel, but we are to be alert at all times, day or

night, and be ready to pray for anyone who needs it. The message Paul is trying to impart here is a message of compassion and care among the saints. We are to love and care for one another at all times and in all situations. What concerns you concerns me. My problem is your problem. And our neighbor's crisis is our crisis.

This is an impossible standard to achieve until we add the phrase "in the Spirit." Watching, persevering prayer is praying in the Spirit. There is no way we can come into oneness and unity apart from the Holy Spirit. And apart from the Holy Spirit, our prayers are lifeless and powerless — and so are we! To continue to pray fervently and passionately until we get the victory we must allow the Holy Spirit to be our inspiration, strength, and guide.

Paul wrote to the Romans that there will be times when we have no idea what to pray, but the Holy Spirit will take care of the matter:

> Likewise the Spirit also helpeth our infirmities: for we know not what we should pray for as we ought: but the Spirit itself maketh intercession for us with groanings which cannot be uttered.
>
> And he that searcheth the hearts knoweth what is the mind of the Spirit, because he maketh intercession for the saints according to the will of God.
>
> ROMANS 8:26-27

At times we may feel vulnerable, confused, and inept as we face certain situations in our lives. We may even look vulnerable to others. But if we will pray in the Holy Ghost and be filled with the Holy Ghost, we will not stay vulnerable! The more we pray in the Spirit, the stronger we experience the anointing, or the tangible presence and life-changing power of the Spirit. It is the anointing that breaks every yoke of bondage and sets us and others free. It is the Holy Spirit who empowers our prayers and brings them to the effective, devil-crushing level of fervency, and we know from James 5:16 that the "effectual fervent prayer" is the prayer that availeth much!

TOGETHER WE STAND

Praying always with all prayer and supplication...for all saints.

EPHESIANS 6:18

Notice that Paul does not say, "Now all you *intercessors*, pray," nor did Jesus tell Joshua, "Now just take the ones who can pray to march around the wall." No! The whole nation of Israel marched around Jericho — men, women, and children. God commands *all* believers to pray! I believe the call of

God to the Church today is a call to prayer, both to the individual believer and to the corporate body.

It's a known fact that war is one of life's great equalizers. We often see the dismissal of prejudice and bigotry in the middle of a war. No soldier in a foxhole cares what color a fellow soldier's skin is — he only cares whether that soldier is on his side. Blacks who have never cared for whites and whites who have never cared for blacks have left foxholes as friends. A prejudiced person might say after the war is over, "Oh, I can't stand people of that color or that race," but then they usually add, "except for Fred. Fred is all right. Fred isn't like the rest of them. Fred is a good brother." And the reason Fred isn't like "the rest of them" is solely because Fred was on their side in the foxhole of battle!

In chapter 2 of Ephesians, we saw how God brought Jew and Gentile together in Christ Jesus. In Christ, believers of all shapes, colors, sizes, ethnic groups, and cultures have a common enemy, and it's God's desire that we come together. More-over, it is a necessity that we come together in order to win the war against Satan and his demonic forces of evil.

When Paul wrote to the Ephesians, the large shields used by the Roman soldiers at that time could be locked together in such a way that an entire row of soldiers could move forward as a single unit, fully protected. It probably looked like a moving wall. The protection over each soldier multiplied because of this union, but so did their power and ability to move forward and conquer.

What an awesome picture of corporate prayer in the Church! We do not stand alone. We do not fight alone. We are to fight as a united front taking on the enemy and standing strong against him both for each one of us individually and for the body as a whole. As we join our faith with one another in prayer, the power of God to save, heal, deliver, and set free is multiplied hundreds of thousands — even millions — of times over!

We need to be unified and organized as a fighting force because the enemy is unified and organized. When Jesus encountered a demon-possessed man in the country of the Gadarenes, He asked him, "What is your name?" And the man replied, "Legion." (See Luke 8:26-36.) "Legion" not only refers to the fact that there were many demons in this man, but it is a military term that also means those demons were an organized stronghold in him. Those demons were fulfilling their assignment and working with the other demons to hold this man in bondage.

The Bible tells us that one believer may send a few demons to flight, but two in prayerful agreement send many demons to flight. As we read in Leviticus 26:8, "Five of you shall chase an hundred, and an hundred of you shall put ten thousand to flight." Being locked together in prayer, praying in faith as a body, releases the multiplied power of God against the enemy.

There are times when we are alone in the lions' den and God delivers us. Then there are times when we are with our buddies in the fiery furnace and our collective faith brings us through. In most situations, however, we need each other because God planned it that way. We need Him and we need each other to succeed. We are not a loose group of lone rangers, each one doing their own thing. We are the family of God.

The family who prays together, stays together. And the family who stays together conquers the land!

8

THE POINT
OF IT ALL

Obey your parents in the Lord.

Do not provoke your children to wrath.

Servants, obey your masters.

Masters, treat your servants with respect and kindness.

Do all things as unto the Lord and look to Him for your reward.

Be strong in the Lord and in the power of His might.

Know your enemy: Hate the devil and love the people.

Put on truth: Get honest with God and purify your life.

Put on righteousness: Know who you are in Christ.

Put on peace: Line your will up with God's will.

Put on faith: Trust God in all things at all times.

Put on salvation: Rejoice in your redemption and rise to the stature of Jesus Christ.

Put on the Word of God: Believe and speak only the living, life-transforming Word of God.

Have an attitude of prayer at all times for all the saints.

Pray individually and corporately until God's will is accomplished.

After the war has been won, then what? Here are Paul's closing words to the Ephesians:

> *Peace be to the brethren, and love with faith, from God the Father and the Lord Jesus Christ.*
> *Grace be with all them that love our Lord Jesus Christ in sincerity. Amen.*

EPHESIANS 6:23-24

There is the peace that leads us through the battle, but then there is another *peace* afterward. When victorious, conquering peace fills our hearts, stays our minds, and encompasses our being, we know the battle has been won. This is not a fleeting peace, but an abiding peace, a peace that is beyond rational explanation. It's real and it's pervasive. It floods our being and spills out onto everyone we touch.

There is the love that binds us together as a warrior bride in the heat of battle, but there is another *love* afterward. Love bursts forth from our innermost being upon defeating the enemy of our souls. We grin at one another, our eyes shining with the unspoken understanding that we fought as one, laid down our lives for our Lord and one another, and now live to shout the victory together.

There is the faith that moves us on when we can go no farther, but there is another *faith* afterward. A deep, abiding faith comes from having witnessed the massive wall of Jericho tumble to the ground. Turning from the scene of our incredible, unimaginable miracle, we gaze into the eyes of our Captain, tears running down our faces. Before the wall fell, we chose not to doubt Him. After the wall falls, we wonder why we doubted in the first place.

This victory, this peace, this love, and this faith have come "from God the Father and the Lord Jesus Christ." After the battle is won, our hearts overflow with love and worship. Peter said in his second letter that grace and peace are multiplied through the knowledge of God, or to the degree to which we become intimate with Him. (See 2 Peter 1:2.) After all is said and done, when the war is won and the enemy has been buried, we finally have the *grace* to "love our Lord Jesus Christ in sincerity."

"Sincerity" means without corruption. We are holy as He is holy and we love Him wholly. We love Him with our whole heart, soul, mind, and strength. And we realize… that was His point all along as He brought us through all the facets of our life in Him.

We marvel at His wealth.

We are His workmanship.

We worship Him.

We walk in Him.

We are wed to Him.

We do warfare with Him.

And in the end, we are His people and He is our God!

REFERENCES

Adam Clarke Commentary. 6 vols. Adam Clarke. *PC Study Bible.* Version 2.1J. CD-ROM. Seattle: Biblesoft, 1993-1998.

Barnes' Notes on the OT & NT. 14 vols. Albert Barnes. *PC Study Bible.* Version 2.1J. CD-ROM. Seattle: Biblesoft, 1993-1998.

The Bible Knowledge Commentary: An Exposition of the Scriptures. Dallas Seminary faculty. Editors, John F. Walvoord, Roy B. Zuck. Wheaton, IL: Victor Books. 1983-1985. Published in electronic form by Logos Research Systems Inc., 1996.

Brown, Driver, & Briggs' Definitions. Francis Brown, D.D., D. Litt., S. R. Driver, D.D., D. Litt., and Charles A. Briggs, D.D., D. Litt. *PC Study Bible.* Version 2.1J. CD-ROM. Seattle: Biblesoft, 1993-1998.

Dressed to Kill. Rick Renner. Tulsa, OK: Albury Publishing, 1989.

Expositor's Bible Commentary, New Testament. Frank E. Gaebelein, General Editor. J. D. Douglas, Associate Editor. Grand Rapids, MI: Zondervan Publishing House, 1976-1992.

A Greek-English Lexicon of the New Testament and Other Early Christian Literature. Walter Bauer. Second edition, revised and augmented by F. W. Gingrich, Fredrick Danker from Walter Bauer's fifth edition. Chicago and London: The University of Chicago Press, 1958.

The Greek New Testament. Editor Kurt Aland, et al. CD-ROM of the 3rd edition, corrected. Federal Republic of Germany: United Bible Societies, 1983. Published in electronic form by Logos Research Systems, Inc. 1996.

Greek (UBS) text and Hebrew (BHS) text. *PC Study Bible.* Version 2.1J. CD-ROM. Seattle: Biblesoft, 1993-1998.

The Hebrew-Greek Key Study Bible. Compiled and edited by Spiros Zodhiates, Th.D. World Bible Publishers, Inc., 1984, 1991.

Interlinear Bible. PC Study Bible. Version 2.1J. CD-ROM Seattle: Biblesoft, 1993-1998.

Jamieson, Fausset & Brown Commentary. 6 vols. Robert Jamieson, A. R. Fausset, and David Brown. *PC Study Bible.* Version 2.1J. CD-ROM. Seattle: Biblesoft, 1993-1998.

A Manual Grammar of the Greek New Testament. H. E. Dana, Th.D. and Julius R. Mantey. Toronto, Canada: MacMillan Publishing Company, 1927.

Matthew Henry's Commentary. 6 vols. Matthew Henry. *PC Study Bible.* Version 2.1J. CD-ROM. Seattle: Biblesoft, 1993-1998.

The New Linguistic and Exegetical Key to the Greek New Testament. Fritz Reineker, Revised version by Cleon Rogers and Cleon Rogers III. Grand Rapids, MI: Zondervan Publishing Company, 1998.

Strong's Exhaustive Concordance of the Bible. J. B. Strong. *PC Study Bible.* Version 2.1J. CD-ROM. Seattle: Biblesoft, 1993-1998.

Vincent's Word Studies in the NT. 4 vols. Marvin R. Vincent, D.D. *PC Study Bible.* Version 2.1J. CD-ROM. Seattle: Biblesoft, 1993-1998.

Wuest's Word Studies from the Greek New Testament for the English Reader. Volume One, Ephesians. Kenneth S. Wuest. Grand Rapids, MI: Wm. B. Eerdmans Publishing Company, 1953.

ABOUT THE AUTHOR

T. D. Jakes is the founder and senior pastor of The Potter's House church in Dallas, Texas. A highly celebrated author with several best-selling books to his credit, he frequently ministers in massive crusades and conferences across the nation. His weekly television broadcast is viewed nationally in millions of homes. Bishop Jakes lives in Dallas with his wife, Serita, and their five children.

To contact T. D. Jakes, write:
T. D. Jakes Ministries
International Communications Center
P. O. Box 210887
Dallas, Texas 75211

or visit his website at:
www.tdjakes.org

Loose That Man and Let Him Go!

(special gift edition)

Just for Men!

Includes 64 inspiring and motivational devotions written specifically for men. The perfect gift for any man—any time of the year.
AP-086
$16.99

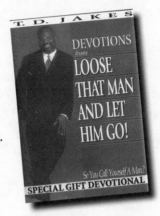

Woman Thou Art Loosed

(special gift edition)

Great "anytime" gift for any woman!

The bestselling devotional, now in an exquisite cloth-bound gift edition! Daily devotions developed from the bestselling book by T. D. Jakes. The perfect gift for every woman, this cherished volume of hope and expectancy will be treasured and lovingly passed on for generations to come.
AP-085
$16.99

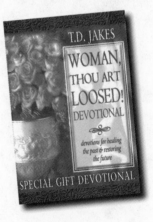

Six Pillars for the Believer *(video 1)*

First in the Series

In chapter one of Ephesians, The Apostle Paul helps us discover who we are, whose we are, what we have, and how to receive all the spiritual blessings that God has prepared for us as His children.

AP-146

$19.99

Six Pillars for the Believer *(video 2)*

Second in the Series

In chapter two of Ephesians, The Apostle Paul teaches us about our resurrection out of sin and death and how we can learn to walk with Christ in fullness of joy. Bishop Jakes encourages us to help others receive the wealth and blessing of God.

AP-147

$19.99

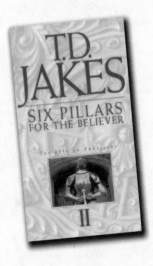

Six Pillars for the Believer *(video 3)*

Third in the Series

In chapter three of
Ephesians, Paul gives us a
brief autobiography. We
learn in this chapter that
Paul considers himself a slave
for Christ. Bishop Jakes gives
tremendous insight into
Paul's background and holds
him up as an example of
forsaking self and focusing on
Christ.
AP-148
$19.99

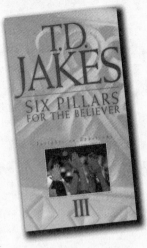

Six Pillars for the Believer *(video 4)*

Fourth in the Series

In chapter four of
Ephesians, Paul shows us
how to pursue the calling
that God has for each of
us, and he motivates us to
move on to the next level.
Bishop Jakes exhorts us,
saying our walk as believers
should be a divine reflection
of our unique calling.
AP-149
$19.99

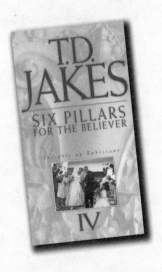

Six Pillars for the Believer *(video 5)*

Fifth in the Series

In chapter five of Ephesians, Paul challenges us to not just walk in love, but to follow Christ's example and love others just as He loved us. Bishop Jakes points out that Paul's desire was for Christians to demonstrate outwardly what God had done inwardly.

AP-150
$19.99

Six Pillars for the Believer *(video 6)*

Sixth in the Series

In chapter six of Ephesians, Paul deals with our relationships with others and how we are to submit ourselves to God and to others. Bishop Jakes speaks in depth on God's desire concerning how we manage our own house and gives several powerful principles for parents.

AP-151
$19.99

T.D. Jakes Speaks to Men

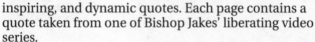

Power-Packed Quotes for Men

T.D. Jakes' portable for men is packed with motivational, inspiring, and dynamic quotes. Each page contains a quote taken from one of Bishop Jakes' liberating video series.

AP-986
$6.99

T.D. Jakes Speaks to Women

Life-Changing Quotes for Women

As you read each quote in this inspirational portable, you will be challenged, comforted, healed, and set free! Bishop Jakes' message is clear—that no matter where you have been or what you have done, God has forgiven you and wants to heal your past so you can change your future.

AP-987
$6.99

Lay Aside the Weight

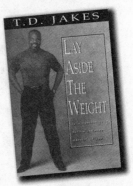

*T.D. Jakes shares the way
to a new you!*

Discover the same nutritional,
weight-loss secrets and discipline techniques that Bishop
Jakes incorporated into his life.
Take control! Using the five
steps outlined in this dynamic
book, you will learn how to
shed unwanted weight in every
area of your life. Includes a
complete section of weight-fighting recipes!
AP-035
$19.99

Lay Aside the Weight
(workbook & journal)

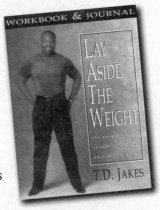

Step by Step!

The best way to get the most
out of T.D. Jakes' bestselling
book, *Lay Aside the Weight,* is
to make it applicable to your
own life. Now it's even easier
to do just that! This extensive
workbook and journal enables
you to focus on the specific
health information you need
to be completely successful in
your health and weight-loss
plan.
AP-083
$11.99

Woman Thou Art Loosed

*The One
That Started it All!*

This book has changed hundreds of thousands of women and continues to grow in popularity. This beautiful hardcover edition makes a great gift for a loved one, friend, or even you!
AP-985
$19.99

Woman, Thou Art Loosed! *(devotional)*

Bestseller now a Devotional

This insightful devotional was created for the thousands of women from around the world that have received healing and restoration through the *Woman, Thou Art Loosed!* message. Each liberating chapter is designed to assist you in keeping the binding chains of the past from refastening themselves in your life.
AP-020
$13.99

So You Call Yourself a Man?

Bestselling Devotional for Men

Written in the charismatic style that T.D. Jakes is know for, this devotional for men continues to be a bestseller year after year. Be challenged through the lives of ordinary men in the Bible who became extraordinary, and let God use your life to accomplish extraordinary things.

AP-026
$12.99

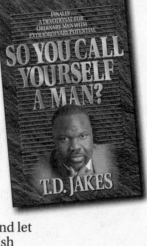

Loose that Man & Let Him Go! *(paperback)*

Over 250,000 sold!

Within the pages of this book begins the healing of fathers and sons. God's Word will release the empty, nagging ache of unresolved conflicts, and men will learn how to turn their pressures into power as they bask in the revelation light of God's plan.

AP-915
$13.99